PROHIBITION
IN
COLUMBUS
OHIO

Visit us at
www.historypress.net
....
This title is also available as an e-book

ABOUT THE AUTHOR

 lex is a former archaeologist and a local historian. He is a lifelong resident of Columbus, where he lives with his wife, Erin, and son, Lincoln.

PROHIBITION

IN

COLUMBUS

OHIO

ALEX TEBBEN

AMERICAN PALATE

Published by American Palate
A Division of The History Press
Charleston, SC
www.historypress.net

First published 2017

Manufactured in the United States

ISBN 9781467137218

Library of Congress Control Number: 2017940944

Erin, RHMILY

CONTENTS

INTRODUCTION

Columbus, Ohio, is many things—the capital of Ohio, Arch City, Test Market USA and home of the Ohio State Buckeyes. Hard drinking has never been one of Columbus's claims to fame. The word *prohibition* conjures up images of gangsters, daring car chases with bootleggers and glamorous speakeasies. Rarely does it make you think of the city of Columbus. That is not to say that Columbus did not have its bootleggers, speakeasies and occasional run-ins with the mob, because it did, but the story of prohibition in Columbus is about so much more—it is actually many different stories.

Prohibition did not happen overnight. There was no sudden consensus that the country needed to stop drinking. The fight for prohibition lasted generations. The story of prohibition in Columbus is the story of the temperance movement, the women's groups that crusaded for decades to end the scourge of the drink and the Anti-Saloon League, all of which finally brought about the victory over alcohol. Even though brewing beer was never a terribly large industry in Columbus, the story of prohibition in Columbus is the story of the brewers and how they shaped their neighborhood.

This story did not end in 1933 with the repeal of the Eighteenth Amendment. It continued, relating the trials of a neighborhood trying to rebuild after being ravaged by prohibition. It is also the story of how, eighty years later, Columbus has seen a resurgence in breweries and distilleries, helping to bring back its drinking culture.

CHAPTER 1

THE TEMPERANCE MOVEMENT

Prohibition in Columbus started in May 1919, but to start our story there would be a disservice to the generations of men and women who fought to get there. Ohio was a center for the temperance movement decades before national Prohibition became a reality.

One of the greatest challenges for anyone advocating for temperance was that there were few alternatives to alcohol. Columbus did not get filtered water until 1908.[1] Before water filtration became widespread, alcohol was actually viewed as being a healthy alternative to water. Water could carry disease; in fact, Columbus had frequent outbreaks of cholera due to tainted water.[2] Brewers would frequently promote their drinks as a healthier option than water. In one advertisement in 1878, the Born Brewing Company claimed:

> *No one can dispute the fact that beer possesses more nutrition than any other drink in use....A beer drinker will never become a drunkard if he leaves whisky alone. Nine doctors out of every ten will recommend beer to the consumptive, when all other medicines have failed, and many has it saved from an early grave by its invigorating and life giving qualities. Temperance advocates, in their enthusiasm lose sight of the fact that beer is health, and seek to abolish the manufacture. It is an erroneous idea, and like all other ideas formed in an enthusiastic frame of mind, will depart in time like drifting smoke before an idle wind.*[3]

STEP 5.
The summit attained
Jolly companions
A confirmed drunkard.

STEP 4.
Drunk
and
riotous.

STEP 6.
Poverty
and
Disease.

STEP 3.
A glass
too
much.

STEP 7.
Forsaken
by
Friends.

STEP 2.
A glass to
keep the
cold out.

STEP 8.
Desperation
and
crime.

STEP 1.
A glass
with
a Friend.

STEP 9.
Death
by
suicide.

THE DRUNKARDS PROGRESS.
FROM THE FIRST GLASS TO THE GRAVE.

Typical of the types of images that temperance groups produced, *The Drunkards Progress*, by Currier & Ives, shows man's descent into alcoholism and, eventually, death. *Courtesy of the Library of Congress.*

When the temperance movement began, it was clear that the brewers had the advantage. Although the brewers held on to the advantage for years, they would eventually lose it.

Ohio's first statewide temperance organization began in 1852, almost seventy years before Prohibition, in the most unlikely of places. In January 1852, in the pages of the Columbus-based *Ohio Cultivator*, a semimonthly newsletter that was "devoted to agriculture, and horticulture and domestic and rural economy,"[4] came a call from Josephine Cushman Bateman, wife of the magazine's editor, Michael Bateman, for a women's state temperance society. There had been local temperance organizations for years, but this was the first attempt to organize a statewide organization.

Mrs. Bateman called on all the local organizations to send delegates to Columbus the next January, where together they would "form phalanx after phalanx…in this great good work."[5] The first meeting of the State Women's Temperance Society of Ohio was held in January 1853. The reason behind the organization was that "women are the greatest suffers of the effects of intemperance, it is their right, and not only their right, but an imperative as mothers, daughters, and sisters to act individually and collectively, to petition and remonstrate in every laudable way to discountenance the use of alcoholic drinks."[6] It was resolved that they would seek to model the temperance movement in Ohio on that of Maine. In the so-called Maine Law, the state of Maine had passed a statewide prohibition against the sale of intoxicating drinks. The society resolved to lobby its "male friends" to vote for those who would support for Ohio the same sort of law that passed in Maine.[7]

There was a common thread here that ran throughout the entire fight for state prohibition. Initially, it was women who led the fight to ban alcohol. It was mostly men at the time who were the main drinkers, yet it was seen as the women's role at the time to raise the children to lead morally sound lives. At the second meeting, the society further elaborated its plan. It was resolved that the fight for temperance was bigger than loyalty to any political party and that they could not support any candidate who did not back prohibition.[8] With the gifts of hindsight, we can see that the methods proposed in the 1850s were quite similar to those that would be embraced, ultimately to victory, by the Anti-Saloon League. We also know that the State Women's Temperance Society of Ohio was destined to fail in its mission. History threw a curveball at the society: the Civil War.

During the bloody conflicts of the Civil War, temperance simply was just not a pressing issue. Because of this, many temperance organizations did make it to the end of the war, the State Women's Temperance Society among them.[9] Abolitionism also took some of the wind out of the temperance movement's sails. During the war, the Republican Party sought to gain the support of newly arriving German immigrants in its antislavery efforts. Germans had long been a target of the temperance movement due to the fact that many of the large breweries had been established by German immigrants. The Republicans decided that they would not risk alienating the Germans to appease the temperance groups—ending slavery was much more important than ending drinking. The leader of the American Temperance Union was told by Republican leaders that "temperance, for humanity's sake must yield,"[10] and yield it did. The temperance movement stumbled during the 1860s, and many groups folded. In Columbus, though, the number of breweries actually increased during the war.

In the wake of the Civil War, it took almost a decade for the temperance movement in Ohio to regain its feet. There were many temperance organizations that began during the 1870s. The Prohibition Party, which, as its name implies, was a political party devoted to trying to bring about Prohibition, held its first national convention in Columbus in 1872. The Prohibition Party demonstrated a new method of agitating for Prohibition. Unlike the previous temperance organizations, the Prohibition Party did not seek to work within the traditional parties to bring about incremental change.[11] Although the Prohibition Party never achieved any real successes at the ballot boxes, it did help to ensure that temperance was kept in the national spotlight.

Chapter 2

THE WOMEN'S CRUSADE AND THE WCTU

The Prohibition Party was not the only powerful temperance organization that was founded in the early 1870s. The origins of the Woman's Christian Temperance Union (WCTU), which became one of the most powerful temperance organizations, can be traced back to an exact day: December 23, 1873. In an act of temperance agitation that would become known as the Women's Crusade, women in Hillsboro, Ohio, took to the streets, visiting saloons to pray for the patrons and cause general disturbances for saloonkeepers, including asking them to sign pledges to stop selling alcohol.[12]

Matilda Carpenter, the only one of the Crusaders who lived to see national Prohibition, recalled that day. In the crowded saloons, the women read their declaration:

> *Knowing as we do, the fearful effects of intoxicating drinks, we the women…after earnest prayer and deliberation, have decided to appeal to you to desist from this ruinous traffic that our husbands, brothers, and especially our sons, be no longer exposed to this terrible temptation, and that we may no longer see them led into these paths which go down to sin and bring both soul and body to destruction. We appeal to the better instincts of your hearts in the name of the desolate homes, blasted hopes, ruined lives, widowed hearts; for the honor of our community, for our property, for our happiness, for our good name as a town; in the name of God, who will judge you as well as ourselves for the sake of your own souls, which are to*

be saved, or lost, we beg, we implore you, to cleanse yourselves from this heinous sin and place yourselves in the ranks of those who are striving to elevate and ennoble themselves and their fellowmen; and to this we ask you to pledge yourselves.[13]

According to Carpenter, by the end of the week the women had won "unconditional surrender [from the saloonkeepers, and] the success of our campaign...inspired similar crusades in other parts of Ohio."[14] These Crusades started something moving.

The following year, the Crusaders met in Cleveland to form a national front with which to combat the scourge of alcohol. This meeting was the foundation of the Woman's Christian Temperance Union, the most influential member of the temperance movement for the better part of twenty years. At the 1874 convention in Cleveland, Annie Wittenmyer, a leader of one of the Crusades in Philadelphia, was elected the WCTU's first president. Much like earlier temperance organizations, the WCTU believed that temperance was primarily a fight for women because they "enjoyed greater moral strength than men. In Temperance work...men had a tendency to quit the battle, but women persisted."[15] They believed that "the

The Women's Crusade. *Courtesy of the Library of Congress.*

PROHIBITION IN COLUMBUS, OHIO

The Women's Crusade. *Courtesy of the Library of Congress.*

liquor traffic is the greatest curse of our race…draining our financial resources without compensation hoarding up the millions in unholy monopoly collecting them piteously off the poor working vassals of the drink demon."[16] The language may have gotten more fiery since the State Women's Temperance Society of Ohio, but the message was almost the same. While men drank, squandering money in the saloons and condemning their families to live in squalor, the women were responsible for maintaining the moral center of the household.

As president, Frances Willard transformed the WCTU but also controversially allied with the Prohibition Party. *Courtesy of the Library of Congress.*

Its auspicious beginnings aside, we know that the WCTU would not ultimately be successful by itself in its efforts to ban alcohol. Failure for the WCTU would not come from any external forces, such as the Civil War, but from the inside. The WCTU had its own internal struggles that kept it from developing consistent strategies for tackling the alcohol problem. At its founding, the mission of the WCTU was simply to ban alcohol. This single goal gave the organization a definite mission and a unifying point to rally behind. Before long, however, there were differences in opinion about the direction the WCTU should be taking. The first major crisis for the WCTU came in 1879, when Frances Willard was elected president. Willard had a vision for the organization that differed drastically from that of its founders. Curiously, Willard's leadership would, at the same time, turn the WCTU into a powerful national force but ensure that it would not be able to achieve national Prohibition.

Under Willard, the mission of the WCTU began to change in a classic case of mission creep. Originally, the mission had been focused on the one goal of bringing alcohol to an end, but under Willard, it changed into a more amorphous "protection for the American home."[17] Among the causes the WCTU now championed was women's suffrage. If women could vote, they argued, Prohibition would be easier to pass. Although the new causes were noble, the shift in focus concerned Wittenmyer and

Ellen Foster, leader of the breakaway Non-Partisan WCTU. *Courtesy of the Library of Congress.*

other founding members that it might dilute the temperance message and damage their original cause.[18]

For a time, Willard's leadership was wildly successful for the WCTU. Under Willard, the WCTU kept expanding; by 1883, it had more than seventy-three thousand members and groups set up in forty-two states and territories.[19]

In 1884, when the WCTU was at the height of its power, a decision was made that would end up tearing the WCTU apart. Up to this point, the WCTU had made a point to be nonpartisan in that it would support whichever candidate supported dry legislation. In 1884, instead of backing individual candidates, Willard gave the endorsement of the WCTU to the Prohibition Party. Allying itself with the Prohibition Party was a source of internal strife that weakened the WCTU and diminished its role in the struggle for national Prohibition for many years. Many members of the WCTU felt betrayed by the action. They felt that tying themselves to the Prohibition Party took away their agency to make change. The leader of the opposition was Ellen Foster, who was a successful temperance agitator from Iowa. Foster argued that binding themselves to the Prohibition Party would anger their current allies and limit their ability to make progress on their own. It was Foster's concern that women would be less likely to join the WCTU now that the ability to make a difference was taken out of their hands and given to the men of the Prohibition Party.[20] Foster argued that the WCTU should continue its nonpartisan approach by endorsing dry candidates and "follow the banner of prohibition, not politicians."[21]

The infighting in the ranks of the WCTU was devastating. Foster's fears came true: donors did dry up and recruitment did fall off. The Republican Party had generally been more sympathetic to the prohibitionist cause and felt betrayed by the WCTU officially backing the Prohibition Party and subsequently sought the support of other temperance organizations.[22] In 1885, the Ohio branch of the WCTU broke from the national organization to start its own version it dubbed the Ohio Non-Partisan Woman's Christian Temperance Union.

In 1889, the civil war in the WCTU came to a head. At the 1889 WCTU convention, Ellen Foster led a revolt and formally broke from the organization. Foster and her allies met with the Ohio Non-Partisan WCTU to form a new national organization that was based on the original ideals of the WCTU.[23] The National Non-Partisan WCTU endorsed the candidates it felt best aligned with its goals and focused solely on Prohibition. The internal struggles held the WCTU back and helped to create a vacuum in the fight for national Prohibition. In 1893, when the WCTU was still in crisis, a new organization was founded in Oberlin, Ohio, that would fill that vacuum.

CHAPTER 3

THE ANTI-SALOON LEAGUE

No other temperance group had a greater impact on the temperance movement than did the Anti-Saloon League. In the history of the temperance movement, the Anti-Saloon League was "the driving force behind the prohibition movement [and the] first successful single issue advocacy group."[24] Prohibition was largely due to the league's constant agitating, propaganda and influence in Washington. When the organization was founded in 1893, the temperance movement was already almost a century old and was at that time without a leader.

In the 1913 *History of the Anti-Saloon League*, Ernest Cherrington described the world in which the Anti-Saloon League was founded: "[F]or a century and a half…the liquor traffic had been growing by leaps and bounds. For almost one hundred years temperance societies and organizations by the score had spent themselves in a long series of unsuccessful efforts to stem the tide of intemperance. Hundreds of Consecrated men and women, devoted to the temperance cause had given their lives as living sacrifices upon the altar of reform, seemingly without adequate results."[25]

Cherrington's assessment was not altogether charitable, but not altogether wrong either. The previous groups had been extremely devoted to the cause, but they did not really have any lasting results. Cherrington also wrote, "Thus it was that after more than a hundred years, during which time thousands of earnest Christian temperance people had been hoping and praying for a movement that might unite all

Christian forces against the liquor traffic, there came into existence the Anti-Saloon league."[26] It was quite evident that the Anti-Saloon League was confident of its abilities.

One thing that differentiated the Anti-Saloon League from its predecessors was its single-mindedness. Other temperance organizations had diluted the fight against the liquor traffic by taking up other causes. Under Frances Willard, the WCTU took up the goal of achieving women's suffrage—a noble goal surely, but not one in line with the temperance mission. Of course, the Anti-Saloon League was not above pointing out that it was the only group dedicated solely to temperance, and in 1893, it declared that it was "an answer by an organization of men to the prayers of the women of 1873."[27] Even the Prohibition Party had taken up other social reforms that were completely unrelated to actual Prohibition.

A large part of the success of the Anti-Saloon League came from its ability to find politicians who were sympathetic to the dry cause, a practice we know was originally employed by both the State Women's Temperance Society and the WCTU. Unlike the previous organizations, though, the Anti-Saloon League only needed to find candidates sympathetic to temperance and not a host of other additional reforms. Unlike the WCTU or the Prohibition Party, party politics mattered little to the Anti-Saloon League. The league decided that "the wiser method was the non partisan or omni-partisan political method."[28]

In its quest for Prohibition, the Anti-Saloon League played the long game. It was the organization's view that each election provided an opportunity to get a dry candidate into office. After enough elections, there could eventually be enough dry elected officials to finally make a push for legislation.

Despite the grandiose language from its *History* text, the origins of the Anti-Saloon League were no more auspicious than any other temperance organization. Its immediate predecessor was the Oberlin, Ohio Temperance Alliance, a group founded in 1874, the same year that the WCTU was uniting the temperance movement. The Oberlin Temperance Alliance had a far less ambitious goal than national Prohibition; its goal was simply to get alcohol banned in the village of Oberlin. Despite its more limited goal, the Oberlin Temperance Alliance proved to be an effective temperance agitator. By 1882, it had managed to get a local option law passed for college towns, allowing them to vote themselves dry

Howard Russell. *Courtesy of the Library of Congress.*

if they desired. Notable in this early campaign was that it included sending members to Columbus to meet with legislators.[29] This was the beginning of one of the Anti-Saloon League's most successful strategies: lobbying. In later years, the Anti-Saloon League would establish offices in Washington, D.C., so that it would have access to senators and congressmen.

In 1888, while the WCTU was in the process of imploding, the Oberlin Temperance Alliance, flush with success, set its sights on a larger target. With a local option law for college towns under its belt, the alliance was preparing for a campaign for a bill that would allow local option votes at a township level. Howard Russell was in his senior year as a seminary student at the Oberlin College when he was hired to run the campaign for the local option law.[30] After passage of the law and his graduation, Russell left Ohio to pursue a career as a minister in Kansas. Russell, however, did not forget his time working with the Oberlin Temperance Alliance and was back in Ohio six years later with the mission to create a statewide temperance organization. In 1893, Russell founded the Anti-Saloon League, with the aid of the Oberlin Temperance Alliance. Russell was conscious of the mistakes of the previous temperance organizations and right from the start made it a point to not repeat them. In a nod to

Daddy's in There---

And Our Shoes and Stockings and Clothes and Food Are in There, Too, and They'll Never Come Out.

—*Chicago American.*

WANTED—A FATHER; A LITTLE BOY'S PLEA

JULIA H. JOHNSON

A shy little boy stood peering
Through the door of a bright saloon;
He looked as if food and clothing
Would be thought a most welcome boon.

And one of the men, in passing,
As if tossing a dog a bone,
Asked, "What do you want this evening?"
In a rude and unkindly tone.

"I am wanting"—the boy's lips trembled—
"I am wanting my father, sir."
And he gazed at the little tables
Where the careless onlookers were.

It was there that he saw his father,
But the man only shook his head,
And the boy, with his thin cheek burning,
Ran away with a look of dread.

Oh, the fathers—the fathers wanted!
How the heart-break, and bitter need,
With the longings, deep and piteous,
For the wandering children plead.

May the children's call arouse them,
May the fathers arise and go
With the young souls waiting for them,
For the little ones need them so!

SERIES G. NO. 23.

The American Issue Publishing Co.,
Westerville, Ohio

Right: Anti-Saloon League cartoons tried to turn public opinion against the saloons. *Courtesy of the Westerville Public Library.*

Below: The Lincoln Lee Pledge was given to children by the Anti-Saloon League. *Courtesy of the Library of Congress.*

the troubles facing the WCTU, Russell stated that "temperance people… should take a leaf from the operations of the liquor and brewing interests, who 'do not form a party' but instead exercised their influence over existing political organizations and their members."[31]

From the beginning, the Anti-Saloon League took the stance that it would work with individual politicians, not parties. In organizing the Anti-Saloon League, Russell clearly had a number of influences. He received aid from the Non-Partisan WCTU, which showed in the Anti-Saloon League's single-minded purpose. The Non-Partisan WCTU did more than just influence the mission of the Anti-Saloon League; it also provided moral and material support for the fledgling group. In fact, the Ohio branch of the Non-Partisan WCTU helped Russell create the governing structure for the Anti-Saloon League and provided assistance for finding funding. Ohio Non-Partisan WCTU president Ellen Phinney even helped Russell get in contact with John D. Rockefeller.[32]

The Anti-Saloon League would "officially disregard all but prohibition issues so as to unite that largest possible following to sustain pressure to outlaw the liquor traffic."[33] To achieve his goal of national Prohibition, Russell "molded the League into a well organized entity along the lines of a modern corporation,[34] directed from the top down, with a central office, specialized departments and local but not autonomous branches." The Anti-Saloon League began with four departments: Agitation, which was pretty much the propaganda department; Legislations, which tried to get bills introduced; Law Enforcement, which provided information to law enforcement officials regarding current regulations; and the Financial department, which was charged with raising funds for the organization. Each department was to be led by a paid superintendent who reported to an executive committee. On a local level, churches were considered the greatest recruitment centers for the league. Churches often provided members for local leagues and also much-needed financial support. According to the league, "Church bodies…held in their hands the destiny of the Anti Saloon League.…The League's fight was in reality the fight of the organized church against the organized liquor forces."[35] A large part of spreading the news about the dangers of the saloon was using the church as a soapbox.

Among Russell's early hires for the purpose of helping to build a bridge between the Anti-Saloon League and the church were two men who would later prove indispensable in the campaign for nationwide Prohibition: Purley Baker, a Columbus minister, and Wayne Wheeler, a Methodist layman and fellow Oberlin graduate.[36] In Columbus, the Anti-Saloon League had another ally to help spread the news: Washington Gladden, the most influential pastor in Columbus during the 1890s and a champion of the Social Gospel, the idea that "faith advocated the churches' involvement in the search for a better society."[37] It was Gladden's contention that it was the duty of the church to fight for social improvements, an idea that meshed well with the league leader's thoughts that the church should lead the battle for Prohibition. Initially hostile to the idea of a statewide prohibition, the Anti-Saloon League won Gladden over to the point that he offered the use of his church to the league to help spread the word.[38]

Within a year of its founding, the Anti-Saloon League was able to raise enough funds to move its headquarters from the small town of Oberlin to Columbus and open a new office in Washington, D.C. Among the first order of business for the fledgling league was to build its reputation in the temperance world. In 1894, the league tried to get a bill through the Ohio legislature that would allow for a local option vote in each of Ohio's voting precincts; the bill failed, but the "Anti Saloon League had found a probable footing."[39] Seeing the need to stay relevant, it became the goal of the Anti-Saloon League to get a local option law in each legislative session. The thought behind this was to get an ever-increasing area subject to local option laws—first wards, then townships, then counties and so on until it covered the entire state.[40]

After only two years, the Anti-Saloon League decided that it was time to create a national organization to act as a guide for the state and local leagues. Annie Wittenmyer and Ellen Foster, seeming to have turned their backs on the WCTU, helped with the writing of a constitution for the new national organization, the American Anti-Saloon League.[41] At times, the structure of the league got a bit blurry. The national league initially had its headquarters in Washington, D.C., but eventually moved it to Westerville, Ohio, a suburb of Columbus. The Ohio league remained in operation and also had its headquarters in Westerville.

Being the founding branch of the Anti-Saloon League, the Ohio league had a special relationship with the national league. Working for the Ohio Anti-Saloon League was almost like a training camp for the American Anti-Saloon League. The state league was so successful that by 1913, when the campaign for a national Prohibition amendment was launched, "nine out of every ten of the state superintendents of the Anti Saloon Leagues of several states as well as district superintendents and field secretaries, now numbering several hundred, either received training of experience in League work in the Ohio League, or in a state league organized in the 'Ohio Model.'"[42]

To further blur the lines between the national Anti-Saloon League and the Ohio league was the league's main propaganda source: its newsletter, the *American Issue*. Like many facets of the Anti-Saloon League, the newsletter originated in the Ohio league, only later becoming the propaganda arm of the national league. Until 1907, even though it was officially the newsletter of the national league, the *American Issue* primarily focused on news from Ohio. After 1907, individualized versions of the newsletter were created for the different state leagues.[43]

The strategy of the Ohio league, and later the national league, was to produce incremental changes in the status quo. A small victory against the alcohol trade one year could be the springboard to a larger victory the next year. To do this, the Ohio league tried to get a local option law in front of legislators at every session. This goal served two functions: the first was that it kept the Anti-Saloon League relevant, and the second was that if the laws actually passed, then areas would begin to go dry. The Ohio league decided that if it could get a local option law at even a township level, it could begin to dismantle the stranglehold of the saloon.

By the late 1800s, many saloons were actually owned by the breweries. The breweries often tried to expand their market share by building more saloons, trying to branch out into new neighborhoods and attract new customers.[44] By the end of the nineteenth century, only Pennsylvania, New York and Wisconsin had more breweries than Ohio, and only New York and Illinois had more saloons. In Ohio, there was one saloon per two hundred residents.[45] When the twentieth century began, the Anti-Saloon League in Ohio had not managed to get any more dry bills passed. This does not mean, however, that it was entirely ineffective. The strategy of keeping bills in front of the legislature had worked to help build its reputation.

One would think that at this point, the temperance agitators would realize that they all shared the same goals, but this was not always the case. Cherrington was correct in his assertion that the different temperance groups were often bigger enemies to one another than they were to the liquor traffic. Frequently, the different temperance organizations seemed to lose sight of their goal and succumbed to petty squabbles. During the remainder of Frances Willard's life, there was tension within the WCTU, particularly over the endorsement of the Prohibition Party. The Prohibition Party resented the Anti-Saloon League as a newcomer. By the turn of the century, although the Anti-Saloon League had managed to achieve some success in various states, the Prohibition Party remained completely unsuccessful in its mission. The Anti-Saloon League responded to the criticism from the Prohibition Party by claiming that since the liquor traffic had begun to fight them, it was a clear sign that their strategy was the correct one.[46]

Let's look now at who the temperance groups were actually fighting against. Many of the groups in the temperance movement made claims that they were taking on the liquor traffic. To simply call their opponents the "liquor traffic" is to take away their stories. The so-called liquor traffic was made up of real people. These were individuals who were endlessly vilified by the temperance agitators as greedy corruptors of humanity hell-bent on the degradation of all that was right and moral. But were they? Could the temperance groups be right about them? What did the brewers think about the fight they were dragged into?

CHAPTER 4

THE BREWERS

Temperance groups spent years vilifying the alcohol producers. Unfortunately for the brewers and distillers, they did not take the vilification seriously until it was almost too late. They allowed themselves to be attacked, thinking that it would not hurt their livelihood, though it eventually ended up costing them everything. This was one of the advantages the temperance groups had over the alcohol producers, and it allowed them to control the narrative. No matter what one may think about alcohol, the portrayal of the brewers and distillers by the temperance movement was grossly unfair. The men who made the drink were not in league with the devil; they were simply businessmen trying to make a living for themselves. They were family men and religious men, often regarded as pillars of society. They were men proud of their heritage who were actually trying to improve their new home city. Prohibition in Columbus is the story of the lives of these men and the impact they had on the city.

Brewing has been a business in Columbus for almost as long as Columbus has been a city. In Ohio, Columbus may have been the political capital of the state, but Cincinnati was the brewing capital. While brewing as a profession was never a major economic driver in Columbus, it has been estimated that by the 1890s a few hundred people owed their livelihoods to the breweries in Columbus.[47] Although it was never a major factor on the economy of the city of Columbus as a whole, brewing did have a profound impact on the South End of the city, helping to shape Columbus's German

Village and creating its Brewery District. If you were to take a tour of the area in 1880, it would be clear why the area came to be known as the Brewery District:

> Between 1859 and 1868 five breweries opened, Capital (or Capital City), Scioto, Stokers, Zimmermann's, and Park (or City Park) the last brewery of the era was the new Bavarian founded in 1875, which completed the older section of the front street brewing district....beginning at Livingston and walking down the west side of Front Street, would bring one first to the site of Jacob Silbernagel's home. Next would be Hoster's City Brewery, the largest in town. Continuing south across Liberty Street, one would come to the home of Nicholas Schlee, where also John Blenkner and the children of George M. Schlegel lived. Just south of that house, Born's handsome Capital Brewery would take one's attention for the next thirty paces... Across Front Street from Born's brewery was his large home. Proceeding north, all the way from Beck to Hoster Street one should feel dwarfed by the close expanse of the front wall of Schlee's new Bavarian Brewery. North across Hoster was the Zimmermann home, which at one time was also Zimmermann's Ale Brewery. Next door, and reaching to Blenkner Street, was the Phoenix, formerly the Bavarian. West from Front Street, opposite the Phoenix, ran Liberty Street.[48]

The area in question was only around a mile in length, and with seven breweries in operation, it becomes clear just how profound an impact the brewers had on their neighborhood.

The story of the Brewery District starts in 1834 with the settlement of German immigrant Louis Hoster. Hoster was certainly not the first brewer in Columbus, but he was the first to have any real lasting impact on the city. Hoster was the first to build his brewery in the South End, and this helped to establish it as an area of beer manufacturing and as a home for German immigrants. Over the decades, Columbus saw many brewers come and go, most of

Louis Hoster. *Courtesy of the Columbus Metropolitan Library.*

Hoster also invested in real estate downtown. *Courtesy of the Columbus Metropolitan Library.*

Left: Conrad Christian Born. *Right*: Nicholas Schlee. *Courtesy of the Columbus Metropolitan Library.*

whom had little lasting effect on the city. Other than Hoster, there were three who played significant roles in the story of brewing in Columbus: Conrad Born, Nicholas Schlee and August Wagner.

In 1836, a decade and a half before the State Women's Temperance Society began its agitating in Columbus, German immigrant Louis Hoster and his two partners established the City Brewery. Hoster was the first major brewer in Columbus, and his brewery was the largest in the city until the advent of Prohibition. Eventually, Hoster's brewery became one of the top five largest breweries in the nation.[49] In the years before the Civil War, two new breweries, which would eventually be Hoster's main competitors, opened: Joseph Schlegel's (later Nicholas Schlee's) Bavarian Brewery in 1849 and Conrad Born's Capital Brewery in 1859.[50]

It was during this period that the Brewery District began to develop its distinct image. Two factors played key roles in the growth of the Brewery District during the 1860s: an increasing number of German immigrants coming to the city and the sidelining of the temperance movement as the effort to eradicate slavery took precedence over the fight to outlaw alcohol. Because of the increase in immigrants, there was an increase in the number of breweries and employees for the breweries. The homes

The Great Southern Hotel. *Courtesy of the Columbus Metropolitan Library.*

of these employees were usually located within walking distance of the breweries. Because of this, it is easy to see how the breweries became the center of the neighborhood.

Let's go back to our tour: "South of there [Born's Capital Brewery], both sides of the street were lined with houses, many occupied by the families of the Brauarbeiters, the brewery workmen [and] Liberty Street was an integral part of the Brewery District, for its south side was lined with the small homes of the brewery [workers]."[51] The homes of the workers gave the area its distinct look, as they were "homes [that] resembled the working class homes left in Germany: brick, one to one and a half stories, with gables facing the street. Built on limestone foundations, the homes were simply adorned with stone lintels and rectangular tall windows."[52] Houses such as these were common in the Brewery District and farther east in the area now known as German Village. It was due in part to the distinctiveness of the homes that later there would be efforts to preserve the area.

The 1870s proved to be the high-water mark for the number of individual breweries in the city of Columbus. From the 1870s until the first decade of the twentieth century, the number of breweries actually decreased. The decrease was not, however, a result of the temperance movement. Advances in technology were the culprit. During this time, there were huge advancements made in refrigeration, malting and bottling, all of which allowed for massive increases in production if the breweries were able to make the adaptations. Adapting the new technologies was expensive, and many of the breweries simply could not afford to make the leap. Those that were unable to make the changes were incapable of competing with the larger breweries that had.[53] Because of this, many breweries were not able to survive the 1880s and '90s. Those that did—like the City Brewery, the Capital Brewery and the Bavarian Brewery—were able to see a 1300 percent increase in production over the levels from 1870.[54] Although the number of breweries decreased during this time, it does not mean that there were no new ones opening. In 1898, the Columbus Brewing Company was founded.

The breweries that did make the transition were completely transformed. In 1866, Schlee, who took over the Bavarian Brewery in 1860, built a new "grand, splendid" brewery.[55] In the 1880s, he turned the old Bavarian Brewery, which was at the time operated by his stepsons under the name the Phoenix Brewery, into a malt house for the New Bavarian.[56] Born added a refrigeration and bottling plant to the Capital Brewery.[57] Hoster outdid them all, though. The City Brewery added a boiler plant, an icehouse and stables.[58] For the brewers who could afford to expand, business was good. The expansions of the breweries meant that they could employ many more people. By the turn of the century, there were more than five hundred individuals employed by the breweries.[59] These were not just brewers

Business cards from the L. Hoster Brewing Company showed off just how big the brewery had become. *Courtesy of the Columbus Metropolitan Library.*

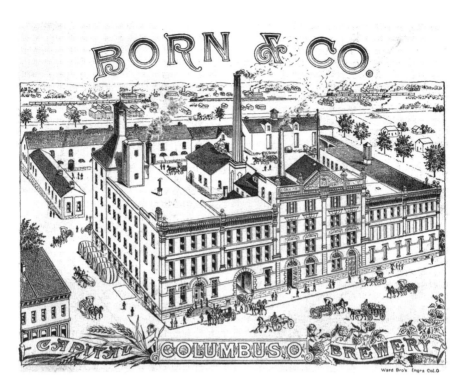

Born's Capital Brewery. *Courtesy of the Columbus Metropolitan Library.*

but also firemen, engineers, stablemen and others, all of whom would be suddenly out of work if the temperance movement won.[60] Most of these individuals lived near the breweries, and if the breweries went under, an entire neighborhood would suddenly be unemployed.[61]

The temperance movement would have everyone believe that the men who ran the breweries were actively doing the work of Satan. This portrayal was decidedly unfair. The brewers were clearly not spending their time diabolically scheming up ways to poison civilization. The brewers were simply men who were trying to make a living in a new city that they happened to care for a great deal. Many of the brewers had immigrated to the United States from Germany, bringing brewing and drinking culture with them to their new home. They were people who loved their city and were often deeply ingrained in its social and cultural life. The brewing community in Columbus was a small world. The brewers lived close to one another, frequently training with or being trained by one another. Sometimes the families would even intermarry. Many of the brewers were also engaged in other businesses not related to brewing. For the latter half of the nineteenth century, there were three main families who ran the largest of the breweries in Columbus: the Hosters, the Borns and the Schlees.

Louis Hoster was a far cry from the caricature of a brewer that the temperance movement so often portrayed. Far from appearing to be an agent of Satan, of Hoster an acquaintance once said, "I have never known a more perfectly honorable man or a more perfect gentleman....He made every cent of his fortune honestly, and he was a model citizen in every way."[62] At his death, it was noted of Hoster that he "was not just a citizen of Columbus, he was in many ways Columbus itself."[63] Hoster did not begin his career as a brewer; rather, he was a wholesaler. It was a chance meeting with another German immigrant that led to a position in one of downtown Columbus's small breweries.

In the space of a year, Hoster went from knowing nothing about brewing to opening a brewery of his own with two partners.[64] He tried very hard to give back to the city that he made his home. Hoster went so far as to become a member of the Columbus City Council from 1849 through 1857. During the Civil War, Hoster spearheaded efforts to send aid to the Union forces.[65] Hoster was also a businessman interested in ventures other than beer, including leading a group that built the first woolen mill in the city.[66] In 1866, Hoster stepped down from his brewery, handing it over to his sons, but he did not abandon his commitment to the city of Columbus, as he served on the Columbus Board of Education for four years from 1869 through 1873. He was also a member of the Columbus Board of Trade and served on the board of the Columbus Machine Company.[67]

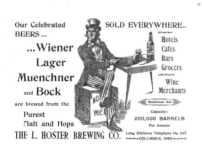

Hoster advertisements. *Courtesy of the Columbus Metropolitan Library.*

Brewing in Columbus was often a family business. When the City Brewery was incorporated in 1885, the Hoster family filled all of the major positions. Louis Hoster remained as president, his son Louis P. was treasurer, son George was the general manager and his nephew, Carl, was the secretary. The younger Hosters worked to maintain the respectability of the family name as members of social clubs and engaging in other civic duties. Louis P. enlisted to fight in the Spanish-American War and was a member of the Columbus Club and the Columbus Board of Trade, among other fraternal organizations.[68] Carl was an Odd Fellow and Druid and a member of German cultural groups. He was also a member of the Independent Protestant Church and "gained high rank among the successful business men and public-spirited citizens of his adopted country."[69] George Hoster, along with his father, was a member of a committee that was responsible for building an independent German Protestant Church, demonstrating their commitment to the religious life of Columbus.[70]

Conrad Born was "one of the pioneer brewers of Ohio for many years and was a prominent and respected citizen of Columbus."[71] Born was the second of the major brewers to settle in Columbus. Born came to Columbus as a trained butcher, not a brewer, and was rumored to have only had ninety-five cents to his name. Although he left the trade, Born maintained his membership in the German Butchers Association; he even held the position of treasurer and was part of the executive committee.[72] Sensing

Louis Phillip Hoster. *Courtesy of the Columbus Metropolitan Library.*

Carl Hoster. *Courtesy of the Columbus Metropolitan Library.*

potential in the Columbus beer market, however, Born decided that it was time to quit the butchery business and opened a brewery. Initially, Born was faced with the problem that he lacked any practical experience in the brewing industry. To learn the trade, Born partnered a former Hoster partner, Jacob Silbernagel, until such time as Born's sons could learn the trade.[73] In 1859, Born and Silbernagel opened the Capital Brewery, which at the time of its opening was even larger than Hoster's.[74]

While it was Conrad Born Sr. who built the brewery, it would be his sons who would transform it. Conrad Born Jr. spent a number of years training at the Moerlein brewery in Cincinnati, eventually marrying a daughter of the proprietor. When Born Jr. returned to Columbus, he partnered with his father and was able to expand the capacity and financial success of the Capital Brewery year after year.[75] Born Jr. was remembered as "one of the best known residents of Columbus, and in his business career has attained notable success."[76] It is not surprising that Born Jr. would be one of the most recognizable citizens of Columbus, as he was very actively engaged in Columbus society. Born Jr. was a member of the Columbus Club and numerous fraternal organizations, including the Elks, Red Men, Odd Fellows and Masons. Many of the temperance groups liked to associate brewers with the devil, which is strange given that they were often deeply religious men who donated frequently to their churches. The recipient of Born Jr.'s largesse was the St. Johns Church.[77]

Christian Born, grandson of Born Sr., followed closely in his father's and grandfather's footsteps. Christian Born was also a prominent member of society in Columbus. He was "vice president of the Columbus Malleable Iron Co., a director of the Hayden-Clinton and Ohio National Banks, a director in the Midland Mutual Insurance Co., the Columbus Academy...a trustee of the Columbus Gallery of Fine Arts and vice president of the Children's Hospital"[78] at the time of his death in 1918. These were not men who reveled in the corruption of civilization but rather were deeply ingrained in the life of Columbus and gave much to contribute to its vibrancy.

The third major brewer in Columbus was Nicholas Schlee. Schlee arrived in Columbus in 1860, a little later than his future rivals. Unlike Louis Hoster or Conrad Born, Nicholas Schlee was, in fact, a trained brewer and had come to take over operations of the Schlegel Bavarian Brewery.[79] Schlee eventually managed to buy out Schlegel and take full control of the Bavarian Brewery. As a boss, Schlee was more generous than his contemporaries and paid his workers eighty-seven dollars per month, which was more than double that of some of the other brewers.[80] Schlee

C. EDWARD BORN
Manager City Sales, The Hoster-Columbus Associated Breweries Company

Conrad Edward, another grandson of Conrad Born Sr., also worked for the Hoster Columbus Associated Breweries Company. *Courtesy of the Columbus Metropolitan Library.*

SURE
TO MAKE
A HIT

Ready for delivery
April 2nd.

Born's BockBeer

Born advertisement. *Courtesy of the Columbus Metropolitan Library.*

also dabbled in other industries as well as brewing, such as real estate and banking. Schlee was the president of the Central Bank and continued to fill that role through various name changes for thirty years.

In addition to brewing, Schlee was also successful in real estate—he owned theaters, apartments and farms. He was also the president of the Great Southern Fire Proof Building and Opera House Company, ownership of which included other leading Germans, including Louis Hoster's grandson. The group built the Southern Hotel, which was a German-style hotel complete with rooftop beer garden, and the attached Southern Theatre.[81] Also a religious man, Schlee was a trustee for the Trinity Lutheran Church, to which he donated the funds to purchase a steeple and three stained-glass windows.[82] Schlee was a generous boss who made a point to give back to his city. After his death, Schlee had his house donated to the Columbus Germania Society, which is an organization dedicated to promoting and protecting German society, so that it could have a proper home. Like Born and Hoster, Schlee demonstrated commitment to his city, not a desire to destroy society.

Let us pause here for a moment to compare the actual lives of the Columbus brewers with the images propagated by the temperance groups. Propaganda published by the Anti-Saloon League does actually portray and suggest that brewers were in league with the devil. Whatever one's feelings about alcohol, this was highly unfair to the Columbus brewers. Do these men seem like folks who were trying to destroy humanity? The story of the brewers of Columbus is the story of men who cared deeply for their city. They cared about their employees, as workers for the brewers were paid better than the average worker in the city.[83] They were engaged with city civics, education, finance and even entertainment by building theaters and sponsoring races at Columbus Driving Park.[84]

CHAPTER 5

NEW BREWERS AND DRY LAWS, 1900–1913

I t is 1900. Our stage is almost set. August Wagner is the only character we have not met yet, but he is waiting in the wings. By 1900, power had begun to shift away from the brewers to the temperance groups. At this point in time, the Anti-Saloon League had been gaining influence with groups and politicians all across the county, the WCTU was still reorganizing from the years under the leadership of Frances Willard and the Prohibition Party had still not accomplished much.

In 1900, there were not many breweries left in the Brewery District: the City Brewery, owned by the Hoster family; the Capital Brewery, owned by the Born family; the Bavarian Brewery, owned by Nicholas Schlee; and the Columbus Brewery. Despite the dearth of breweries, their production levels were more than 1000 percent higher than they had been in 1870. Demand had simply never been higher for their product. Despite the high demand, change was coming. In 1904, the three major brewing companies—Hoster, Schlee and Born—were consolidated, along with the Columbus Brewing Company, into a single company: the Hoster Columbus Associated Breweries Company.[85] The new company was run by George Hoster, with Christian Born as the vice-president. The Born and Schlee breweries remained in existence, for the time being, as part of the Hoster Columbus Associated Breweries Company, and they still made their traditional beers.

Although the breweries in the Hoster Columbus Associated Breweries Company were the only ones in the Brewery District, the city was not without other smaller breweries. The Franklin Brewery opened the same

August Wagner's business card from his time as the brewmaster for Hoster Columbus. *Courtesy of the German Village Society.*

year Hoster merged with Schlee and Born. In 1906, the Gambrinus Brewery, a new brewery, was opened in the Brewery District by August Wagner. Of all the Brewery District brewers, Wagner was the only one who made it through Prohibition. Leading up to Prohibition, Wagner seemed to be better prepared than competitors for the time when their professions would be outlawed. Like the other major brewers, Wagner was also a German immigrant, but unlike Born and Hoster, he was a career brewer. Much like his fellow brewers, though, Wagner was noted as being a model citizen. Wagner, it was said, "stands today at the head of a successful and growing enterprise…and in business circles maintains an enviable reputation for enterprise and integrity."[86] Like Schlee, Wagner also dabbled in real estate, although he tended to buy up properties that held saloons. Beginning his career at the Hoster Company, Wagner worked his way up to being the Hoster brewmaster.

Leaving Hoster, Wagner helped to found the Gambrinus Brewing Company, named after a legendary German king and patron of the brewing arts. Wagner was a feature in many Columbus parades riding a horse and dressed as King Gambrinus. The Gambrinus Brewery even featured a life-size statue of the legendary king on its exterior, modeled on the likeness of August Wagner himself. In an era when the Anti-Saloon League was quickly gaining power, Wagner was able to make a name for himself. In order to bolster his reputation, Wagner entered his beer in contests across Europe and the United States. By winning awards for his beers, Wagner was able to ensure that his brewery had enough name recognition to keep afloat during a time of growing hostility to his trade.

By 1900, the Anti-Saloon League did not yet have any legislative successes, but it had not been idle. The league's luck was going to change quickly. Since its founding, the Anti-Saloon League had been perfecting its methods of endorsing candidates who supported Prohibition. In order to work more

August Wagner dressed as King Gambrinus. *Courtesy of the German Village Society.*

closely with the elected officials in 1889, Edwin Dinwiddie was sent to Washington, D.C., as the legislative superintendent for the league to act as its lobbyist.[87] Validating the methods proposed by Ellen Foster and the Non-Partisan WCTU, the Anti-Saloon League finally managed to propel enough candidates sympathetic to its cause into office in 1902 to successfully pass dry laws for the first time.

That year, the Ohio legislature first demonstrated its sympathy to the temperance movement by passing the Beal Bill. The Beal law allowed incorporated villages and cities to have a local option vote. The Anti-Saloon League would boast that as a result of the bill, ninety-three municipalities in Ohio went dry.[88] This would be a turning point for the Anti-Saloon League—for the first time, it was actually able to inflict real damage to the liquor traffic. The passage of this bill was a blow to the brewers and other wet interests, and it provided proof that the tactics of the Anti-Saloon League were effective. After the Beal law was passed, the production levels of the Columbus breweries began to steadily decrease.

The year 1906, the same year August Wagner and partners opened the Gambrinus Brewery, was the year that the fight for prohibition in Ohio began

Wagner was the model for the King Gambrinus statue outside the Gambrinus brewery.
Courtesy of the Columbus Metropolitan Library.

Above: Advertisement for Augustiner beer. *Courtesy of the Columbus Metropolitan Library.*

Left: Gambrinus advertisement. *Courtesy of the Columbus Metropolitan Library.*

to tip in favor of the Anti-Saloon League. By 1906, the league had gained enough support that it was able to push multiple pieces of legislation aimed at curbing the liquor traffic.[89] Three major pieces of legislation were passed by the State of Ohio that signaled just how strong the Anti-Saloon League had now become. These pieces of legislation were part of a multifaceted attack on the alcohol producers and sellers.

The first was the Aiken tax, which raised the annual tax on a saloon to a nearly prohibitive $1,000. The second was the Search and Seizure law—or, more colorfully, the "Blind Tiger and Speak Easy" law—which made it illegal to ship alcohol into an area that had already voted dry.[90] The third piece of legislation was the Jones Residence District Remonstrance law, which was a local option law that gave the townships and districts in cities the ability to vote dry. The intended effect on the brewing industry was obvious, as each law was intended to hurt the bottom line of the alcohol manufactures and inhibit their ability to do business. The genius was that each law damaged the liquor traffic in a different way.

The Jones local option law was probably the most obvious, as larger areas than before gained the ability to vote dry. The effects of local option laws were immediate—if there were fewer saloons, there would be fewer customers for the brewers. A rapid series of closures would drastically reduce the market for the brewers' products. The Aiken tax nearly tripled the annual tax on saloons from $350 to $1,000. The aim of this tax increase was to make it

The Gambrinus Brewery. *Courtesy of the German Village Society.*

too expensive for saloon owners to continue to operate. Even if it was still legal to operate in some areas, the hope was that by increasing the tax some saloons would close anyway.

In the first years of the twentieth century, the Anti-Saloon League began to argue for stronger law enforcement, a feature that would be consistent throughout the entirety of Prohibition. A curious cooperation developed between the Anti-Saloon League and the Brewers Vigilance Bureau, a

He Can't Put It Out

Public sentiment was going toward the "drys." *Courtesy of the Library of Congress.*

group founded by the Ohio Brewers Association with the goal of cracking down on the illegal abuses of saloons, in which Wayne Wheeler and bureau representatives would patrol local restaurants to ensure that they were not violating any dry laws. The thought on the part of the Brewers Association was that if it kept the saloons in better order, the league would not be able to publish as many damaging articles.[91] It was the belief of Wheeler that the threat of punishment was what was needed to keep people following the laws. Wheeler's penchant for strict law enforcement would serve him well when he left his position of Ohio superintendent to be the legal general counsel for the league in 1915.[92] In 1908, the Anti-Saloon League had another major win: its constant push for local option laws finally got one passed that allowed entire counties to vote dry. By the end of the year, fifty-seven of the sixty-six Ohio counties that took up the issue had voted dry under the Rose law. With entire counties going dry, the Anti-Saloon League demonstrated that it was a very real threat to the continued existence of the brewers. Under the Rose law, more than 1,900 saloons shut their doors in Ohio.[93]

In 1909, the Anti-Saloon League underwent a major change. The national headquarters of the American Anti-Saloon League, the headquarters of the Ohio branch of the Anti-Saloon League and their propaganda arm, the *American Issue*, would all move to Westerville, Ohio. On many levels, the move to Westerville was a strange choice, particularly for the national headquarters. Westerville was a small suburb of Columbus that, up to this point, had only one claim to fame: it was the home of Benjamin Russell Hanby, the composer of "Up On the Housetop." The town, however, did have a few factors that would make it quite attractive to the Anti-Saloon League: the town had been dry for fifty years since a vote in 1859 and the town put up the funds to buy land and build a printing press for the league.[94] The Anti-Saloon League had a new home, and for the first time, the *American Issue* and the national headquarters were located in the same place. The association with the Anti-Saloon League would earn the city of Westerville the nickname the "Dry Capital of the World."[95] Now with its headquarters and propaganda wing consolidated in one place, the Anti-Saloon League would be able to get ready for its next big fight.

Understandably, the brewers had different views on these developments. The brewers finally realized the danger that they were in; however, they still had not managed to create a unified front to defend themselves against the league. They called out Aiken tax as a blatant attempt to shut down legally operating brewers, but nothing came of it.[96] The Jones law was labeled "the most outrageous and miserable law ever passed by the Ohio legislature."[97] Again, little was actually done to try to fight the new laws. There were attempts in Cincinnati to fight the Aiken tax, and brewers in Cleveland protested against the Jones law. In the end, the brewers and saloons lost this round. They were thrown off balance because of the laws and would not be able to regain the ground they lost in 1906. For the first time in the history of the temperance movement, there was a fundamental shift in power away from the wet interests. Inaction on the part of the brewers had cost them the initiative, and from now on they would suffer the consequences.

The Columbus brewers reacted to the changes in their world with relative grace. Being the largest of the Columbus brewers, the Hoster Columbus Associated Breweries Company had actually been able to expand its distribution to states surrounding Ohio, which greatly increased its market share. Incredibly, even as the Anti-Saloon League was obviously gaining power, there were still new breweries opening in Columbus. The Washington Brewery opened in 1907, and the Ohio Brewery opened in

GIVE US——
Columbus Brewing Co.'s SELECT PALE
BOTTLED BEER
NONE SUPERIOR.
PHONE 632.

Columbus Brewery advertisement. *Courtesy of the Columbus Metropolitan Library.*

The Washington Brewery.
*Courtesy of the Columbus
Metropolitan Library.*

the incredibly late date of 1910.[98] Both of them were opened after the vast majority of Ohio counties had already voted dry. It should have been obvious to the brewers that their market was rapidly disappearing. Equally incredible was the fact that the men opening the new breweries were former employees of other Columbus breweries. Both the Washington and Ohio Breweries were opened by former Columbus Brewing Company employees, men who should have been aware of the direction the public was starting to lean regarding alcohol.[99]

CHAPTER 6

THE NATIONAL PROHIBITION CAMPAIGN, 1913–1919

All the battles the Anti-Saloon League had fought before 1913 were really the prelude to the main fight. They were the necessary legwork required to build up the influence and reputation to take the fight to the national level. By 1913, the Anti-Saloon League had so great an influence in Washington that dry congressmen were able to override a presidential veto on a bill that would have prohibited the interstate shipment of liquor into dry areas.[100]

In Columbus in 1913, the Anti-Saloon League announced its plans for the future during its "mammoth twenty year jubilee convention."[101] The league had held annual conventions yearly before, but this time, it was obvious that something was different. In the lead up to the convention, the Anti-Saloon League circulated sample sermons to local churches for what it was calling "Prohibition Sunday," or the day before the convention started. Pastors read the prepared sermons, and the Sunday school teachers signed up students for the Anti-Saloon League's Lincoln-Lee Pledge, in which the students vowed to never partake in alcohol.[102] On convention day, league superintendent Purley Baker and *American Issue* editor Ernest Cherrington made their announcement: from that moment, the league would focus its energy on a constitutional amendment to ban alcohol. Following the Jubilee Convention, the Anti-Saloon League sent members to the Capitol and, in a grand symbolic display, presented to Congress a draft of a resolution for national Prohibition.[103]

Right: Ernest Cherrington.
Courtesy of the Westerville Public Library.

Below: Downtown Columbus just before Prohibition. *Courtesy of the Library of Congress*.

Columbus before Prohibition. *Courtesy of the Library of Congress.*

If this chapter of the story has a star, it is Ernest Cherrington. Cherrington was no stranger to the fight for Prohibition. Long a member of the Anti-Saloon League, he held such positions as the deputy superintendent of Ohio and superintendent of Washington State. A loyal lieutenant in the fight for temperance, Cherrington was called back to Westerville to serve as the managing editor for the *American Issue* in 1908.[104] As the editor of the Anti-Saloon League's newsletter, Cherrington was in charge of the propaganda for the most powerful temperance organization ever seen. Leading the Prohibition amendment propaganda campaign gave Cherrington his chance to shine and also allowed an opportunity to put forth his vision for the future. It was Cherrington's view that Prohibition was not a matter of strictly enforcing laws to obtain obedience but rather of educating people into realizing that abstinence was a better way of life than drinking. Cherrington's vision was that "as more and more citizens witnessed the social benefits of prohibition first hand, they would agree to obey the law as well as seek it."[105]

The Anti-Saloon League's "Golden Jubilee" Convention in Columbus. *Courtesy of the Library of Congress.*

Through his role as editor of the *American Issue*, Cherrington was able to communicate his vision directly to the American public. Cherrington tried to bring his message to the largest possible audience by expanding the number of publications issued by the Anti-Saloon League. Among the new publications, the *New Republic* was used for fundraising purposes, and the *National Daily* was used for getting news from the Anti-Saloon League to the editors of general interest magazines. To help manage the additional publications, Cherrington hired William "Pussyfoot" Johnson, a man who had once led raids on bootleggers as a U.S. marshal.[106] Cherrington's role in the Anti-Saloon League was enhanced by the fact that he was also appointed to the head of its new finance department. The Eighteenth Amendment campaign fueled a massive increase in propaganda and mail in and out of the Anti-Saloon League headquarters in Westerville. Within four years, Westerville would be the smallest town with a first-class post office due to the literal tons of mail generated by the Anti-Saloon League.[107]

The year 1913 was undoubtedly a triumph for the Anti-Saloon League. After the league announced its campaign for national Prohibition, there was no other temperance organization that could challenge its leadership of the temperance movement. Following the announcement of the Eighteenth Amendment campaign, the Anti-Saloon League gained control of the Scientific Temperance Federation, which, led by Cora Stoddard, was an outgrowth of the WCTU's early work to scientifically prove the benefits of temperance. This added a new publication to Cherrington's desk, the *Scientific Temperance Journal*, which continued to push the idea that temperance could be scientifically proven to be better for people and society.

The site where the Anti-Saloon League's propaganda was printed. *Courtesy of the Columbus Metropolitan Library.*

By this point in time, the WCTU had recovered from its infighting and was actually stronger than ever. The age-old rift between the WCTU and the Anti-Saloon League had also healed, and in deference to the more venerable organization, the Anti-Saloon League was conscientious to work with the WCTU on its strategies.[108] The Prohibition Party, on the other hand, still feeling threatened by the Anti-Saloon League, had not realized that it had been supplanted as the leading temperance organization.

As the Anti-Saloon League gained in strength, the brewers were entering a dark chapter in their history. Shortly after the launch of the campaign for

Top: W. "Pussyfoot" Johnson (man standing to the right of two women in hats near the middle). *Courtesy of the Library of Congress.*

Above: Inside the Anti-Saloon League's print shop. *Courtesy of the Westerville Public Library.*

Opposite: The amount of mail the Anti-Saloon League generated gave Westerville a first-class post office. *Courtesy of the Westerville Public Library.*

a Prohibition amendment, events in the wider world played right into the hands of the Anti-Saloon League and would greatly help the organization in its final push against the alcohol industry.

By 1914, entire states were starting to vote themselves dry, and one such state was West Virginia. By this point in time, West Virginia was the main source of income for the Hoster Columbus Associated Breweries. Because much of Ohio had gone dry, the Hoster breweries were already losing hundreds of thousands of dollars in sales every year since 1908.[109] With the loss of West Virginia, half of the sales for the Hoster breweries disappeared, and Hoster, Columbus's oldest remaining brewery, was forced to go into receivership.[110] The company was reorganized as the Hoster Columbus

He Wants the Revenue

Is the Game Worth the Bait?

THE GREEDY BEAST NOW GETS
ONE BOY OUT OF EVERY FIVE.

*"A Saloon can no more run without boys than a grist
mill without wheat." FRANCES WILLARD*

**Are You Dangling Your Boy at the End of a
"Wet Ballot?"**

Anti-Saloon League propaganda.
Courtesy of the Library of Congress.

Company, and control remained in the hands of the Hoster and Born families, as Carl Hoster was the president and Christian Born served as vice-president.[111]

As if the year could not get any worse, in July 1914, due to the assassination of Archduke Franz Ferdinand, World War I began. Although the United States did not enter the war until 1917, its impact would be huge here at home. World War I helped to change the tactics of the fight between the Anti-Saloon League and the brewers. The Anti-Saloon League was not an organization that was squeamish about fighting dirty, and it exploited the war as much as it could. A common tactic before the war that was used by the Anti-Saloon League was to proclaim saloon and brewery owners as being purveyors of poverty and the cause of blight and slums.[112]

During the First World War, the Anti-Saloon League employed one of its most devious and underhanded tactics. In Columbus during the war, it was perhaps not the easiest time to be a German immigrant or of proud German heritage. Anti-German sentiment ran high in Columbus—so high, in fact, that a park not far from the Brewery District in what is now German Village had its name changed from Schiller to Washington Park.[113] During the war, the Anti-Saloon League unapologetically exploited this rampant anti-German sentiment. The Anti-Saloon League believed its fight to be for the very soul of the country and did not hesitate to do whatever it deemed necessary to win. The league's propaganda during the First World War leveled new charges against the brewers. Wrapping itself in patriotism, the Anti-Saloon League was able to pass itself off as a champion of the American way and brewers as traitors.[114] Prohibition had become patriotic; grain, it was argued, was better served going to feed the soldiers in the field instead of being used to make alcohol.[115]

According to the Anti-Saloon League, due to their German heritage, the brewers must be in league with the Germans in the war. Images published

Cora Stoddard. *Courtesy of the Library of Congress.*

by the league show caricatures of brewers, often portrayed as wearing the *pickelhaube*, or German spike helmet, and speaking in broken, German-filled English while slipping money to the kaiser. One cartoon featured an image of Kaiser Wilhelm hiding behind "der beer barrel," actively suggesting that the brewers were engaged in aiding the enemy. It was unquestionably untrue that the brewers in Columbus were secretly agents of the German military or that they wished for Germany to win the war. The brewers were, however, quite proud of their German heritage, which made the attacks by the Anti-Saloon League all the easier. Many of the brewers were members of clubs for German Americans, which through no fault of their own painted convenient targets on them. Nicholas Schlee died the year World War I began and left his home to the Germania Society, which is dedicated to preserving and promoting German song, sport, food and drink.[116]

August Wagner was a member of many German American clubs, including the German-American Society, the Bavarian Society, the Liederkranz, the Germania Singing Society and the Humboldt Society.[117] It was a very low blow by the Anti-Saloon League to call into question the integrity and allegiance of the brewers, who we know cared deeply for their country and city. It was, however, an effective attack. Making villains out of the brewers helped to quickly and negatively change their public image. Because of the war and the relentless onslaught of the Anti-Saloon League, the sympathy of the voters turned to the drys. The debate over Prohibition changed from whether it was morally okay to drink to how it was patriotic to *not* drink.

Upon his death, Nicholas Schlee donated his home to the Germania Society. *Courtesy of the Columbus Metropolitan Library*.

The Anti-Saloon League exploited the First World War as much as it could. *Courtesy of the Library of Congress.*

Wayne Wheeler. *Courtesy of the Library of Congress.*

During the war, Wayne Wheeler was sent to Washington as the national general counsel, working to lobby for and try to craft legislation to favor the dry cause. Toward the end of the First World War, it was Wheeler who led the charge against the brewers, even going so far as to get a Senate investigation into the brewing industry and its German ties.[118] Elsewhere in the league, Ernest Cherrington was working on a new organization, World League Against Alcoholism. It was to be modeled after the Anti-Saloon League and would seek to promote a unified world without alcohol. Expanding the message of the Anti-Saloon League to the world would be a "cause of civic righteousness"[119] for Cherrington.

The period during the First World War was a lean time for the brewers, when they had to do everything they could to stay afloat. One way the brewers tried to keep their costs down was to close inefficient portions of their operations. Product lines were cut and buildings were closed. Because the Hoster Columbus Company had three different breweries, there was much that could be cut. The Capital Brewery, Conrad Born's old brewery, was shut down in 1914, but shuttering this plant still did not make up for the devastating losses.[120] Later, Hoster closed the Bavarian Brewery, Nicholas Schlee's old brewery.[121] By the late 1910s, Hoster had cut its products down to a single beer, called Gold Top. Even extensive cuts were like Band-Aids on gaping wounds—they simply were not enough to stop the losses. The brewers knew that they were going to have to find a way to adapt to the changes in the market or go under.

Oddly enough, one method of adaptation was to actually add new product lines back into production. Shortly before Prohibition, many of the brewers started producing soft drinks. Hoster introduced Bruin hoping that it would be able to stem the tide and cut the drastic losses.[122] Bruin, like many of the other drinks being introduced by the brewers at this time, was a cereal beverage, or "near beer." The goal with cereal beverages was

Leadership of the Anti-Saloon League. *Courtesy of the Library of Congress.*

to make a drink that was so close in taste to actual beer that their longtime customers would still drink it. The beer was brewed and fermented the usual way, and then the alcohol was removed. The addition of the cereal beverage lines may have helped to slow down the losses, but it did not solve the brewers' problems.

During the First World War, the Anti-Saloon League teamed up with the WCTU to engage in a massive lobbying campaign trying to drum up official support for the Eighteenth Amendment. On Capitol Hill, the Anti-Saloon League was successful in getting legislation passed in 1917 that banned the use of grain for distilling.[123] The law, however, did not really please anyone, except maybe the brewers. After a fight over whether brewers should be included in the ban, President Hoover decided that "the availability of beer was essential for the well being of industrial workers."[124] While it could have been seen as a victory, the main effect of the 1917 Lever Bill was to ramp up the Anti-Saloon League's work on getting the Eighteenth Amendment passed.

Left: August Wagner continued to make Hoster's Bruin. *Courtesy of the German Village Society.*

Below: Anti-Saloon League propaganda was ramped up after it launched its Eighteenth Amendment campaign. *Courtesy of the Library of Congress.*

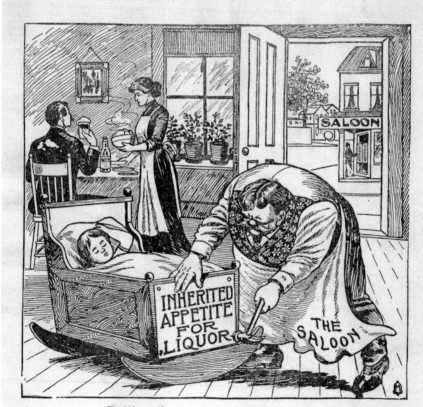

Putting the mortgage on the cradle.

—The Instructor.

Thirty-Six States Can Stop This By
Constitutional Amendment

In 1917, Wayne Wheeler got his draft for the Eighteenth Amendment introduced in the Senate Judiciary Committee.[125] In addition to its public opinion campaign, the Anti-Saloon League mobilized the WCTU to put pressure on the state capitols to back ratification of the Eighteenth Amendment.[126] The last nail in the coffin of the wet cause was the not entirely appropriately named War Time Prohibition Act. Actually passed after the Armistice in 1918, the War Time Prohibition Act was nominally for the purpose of restricting grain for war uses, even though fighting had stopped in November. Peace agreements, on the other hand, were not formally reached until the following June. The act banned brewing on May 1, 1919, and banned the sale of intoxicating beverages on June 30, 1919. With the passage of the act and the Eighteenth Amendment being voted on by the states, the Anti-Saloon League had won.[127] It was obvious even to brewers that the end was coming. Complete national Prohibition was just around the corner.

CHAPTER 7

WELCOME TO PROHIBITION

The ratification campaign for the Eighteenth Amendment proceeded much more quickly than the Anti-Saloon League anticipated. Submitted to the states for ratification in 1918, the last required state ratified the Eighteenth Amendment in January 1919. After the threshold was passed, national Prohibition was set to take effect on January 16, 1920. In Columbus, things were a little different. Columbus voted to go dry on May 27, 1919, nearly seven months earlier than the rest of the nation.[128] Given that Prohibition was orchestrated from the Columbus suburb of Westerville, many of the dry agitators held massive celebrations in Columbus.

In June 1919, the Prohibition Party held its fiftieth anniversary party in Columbus, celebrating the Prohibition victories. Of course, it was living vicariously through the victories of the Anti-Saloon League.[129] In October, the WCTU held the "largest convention in their history"[130] in Columbus. As a symbol of the success of the temperance movement, the gavel used during the meetings at the convention was made from the wood of the church at Hillsboro, where the Women's Crusade began. William Jennings Bryan, himself a longtime temperance agitator, was the keynote speaker at the convention.[131] For the Prohibition groups, it was a time of celebration and jubilation. Many thought that their fight was finally over. But they were very wrong.

It is safe to say that Prohibition in other cities was more glamorous than in Columbus. Columbus had no mob, and our bootleggers were small operators. This does not mean that there were no stories though. Alongside

Golden Hill Distillery. Notice the signs above the door. *Courtesy of the Columbus Metropolitan Library.*

the story of Prohibition has been a story of contradictions between the temperance groups and the liquor trade. On one hand, the Anti-Saloon League would have a person believe that the country had just entered a golden age; on the other, there are tales of crime and corruption. The true story probably lies somewhere in between.

Columbus in 1919 was a city full of change. Following the end of the war, there was a building boom to house the influx of workers who had entered the city during wartime.[132] Just as the face of the city was changing in 1919, so, too, would the lives of its citizens. Prohibition in Columbus is not a story about the city; the city endured just fine.

James Cox, Ohio's governor when it went dry. *Courtesy of the Library of Congress.*

Losing the alcohol trade really mattered very little to Columbus as a whole, as it was never all that large a part of Columbus's overall economy. Instead, Prohibition in Columbus is actually the story of a neighborhood, an industry and individuals.

Prohibition did not sneak up like a thief in the night, and it certainly did not come quietly or unannounced. The protracted battle gave those involved in making or selling alcohol a long time to prepare. Even though Prohibition officially began on May 27, the saloons had to decide whether to purchase a license to continue to sell alcohol after May 25.[133] There were a few different options saloon owners could take in the face of Prohibition. A saloon could simply close, an option many did end up taking, as 276 shut their doors on May 25. Shortly before Prohibition, Columbus had more than 460 licensed saloons in downtown alone.[134] Knowing that Prohibition was right around the corner, many saloons simply ran through their stock before the deadline. Only 9 saloons, plus the bar at the Deshler Hotel, decided to keep selling alcohol until May 27. In theory, this gave them an extra two days of nearly competition-free sales, but some of the saloons also ran out of stock before the time was up.

Prohibition did not necessarily mean that a saloon had to close completely. Even though the saloons could no longer sell alcohol, the businesses were still perfectly allowed to stay open, provided that they convert from saloons to dealers of soft drink. Not only were many saloons bars, but they also served food. Some of these decided to try their luck as just restaurants. Other saloons converted themselves into soda fountains. Some of the new soda fountains simply switched to serving soft drinks, while others whole-heartedly embraced their new role and even added new machinery for the change. Hotels, too, had to shift their priorities. The Neil House and the Deshler Hotel decided to keep their grills open and try to cater to dancers

George Karb was mayor when Columbus went dry. *Courtesy of the Library of Congress.*

instead of drinkers. The New Southern, that grand hotel built by brewer Nicholas Schlee, turned its bar into a barbershop.[135]

A third option that some saloon owners took was to convert the saloons into grocery stores. This might seem like an odd transition, but there were sometimes less savory reasons for such a change. Selling groceries allowed the former saloons access to large amounts of sugar, which could be used in the making of homebrews.[136]

This was a period of real adjustment for the Columbus saloons—some would make it gracefully, and others would not. Some reported a positive change, the sort of change that would make the Anti-Saloon League proud. After a week of Prohibition in Columbus, some former saloons actually reported good business despite the lack of alcoholic sales. "We don't have to make so much as we did under the old system in order to make a fair profit," said one High Street soft drink dealer. "You must remember that liquor carried heavy taxes. Then, too, our goods cost us less than they did in the day when there was a kick in them."[137] There are echoes of the Anti-Saloon League in the quote. It must be remembered that the heavy taxes the former saloon owner complained that he used to have to pay were part of the Anti-Saloon League's effort to squeeze saloons out of business. The

Anti-Saloon League claimed that former saloons like this one were proof that Prohibition was working.

Every year, the Anti-Saloon League issued a *Yearbook*, updating members of the state of Prohibition. Following the passage of national Prohibition, the league's *Yearbook* tried to paint a rosy image of life in Ohio under Prohibition:

> *In most places new business is taking the place of the old saloons such as stores selling candy, buttermilk, men's furnishings, cigars and tobacco, clothing stores, grocery stores and other kinds of business. From our streets the earmarks of the saloon are gone. A larger number of people are being employed in these stores…real estate men report an increased number of homes purchased…deposits in savings banks have increased.*[138]

On one level, the story of Prohibition in Columbus does seem to have played out almost exactly as the Anti-Saloon League said it would. The claims made by the league do appear to have come true on some level. Saloons closing did open up their buildings for new businesses, and often in desirable locations; many of them were, in fact, grocery stores, and home buying did increase. Of course, there was more to the story than the Anti-Saloon League cared to let on.

There was certainly a darker side to Prohibition in Columbus. Not all of the businesses that popped up with the passage of Prohibition were entirely legitimate. There were many entrepreneurial individuals who sought to make their fortunes by subverting the law or through loopholes. At the beginning of Prohibition, it was legal to brew beer for yourself at home. Although it is nearly impossible to tell if this was exactly the case, it has been speculated that many of the former saloons turned grocery stores were fronts for homebrewing operations.[139]

Some individuals were a bit more brazen. On the day Prohibition took effect in Columbus, one enterprising business opened at 527 North High Street. The Columbus Malt and Hop Company sold, as its name implies, malt and hops, the very items that were needed for homebrewing beer.[140] Homebrewing was a popular business in Columbus and was responsible for the success of what eventually became the Wasserstrom Restaurant Supply Company, one of Columbus's most prominent homegrown companies. After his saloon closed down, Nathan Wasserstrom got into the homebrewing business, selling the raw materials for brewing one's own beer. In fact, "the malt and hops business did so well in the 1920s that the company opened 10 branch stores. It sold ten kinds of malt, including two house brands."[141]

Much to the chagrin of the Anti-Saloon League, people did not suddenly stop wanting to drink, or actually drinking, which meant that business for individuals like Wasserstrom was good. Obviously, the Anti-Saloon League was against the brewing of beer at home, as it was a step toward speakeasies. If anyone and everyone could make their own beer, the very foundation of Prohibition would be under threat. Needless to say, the Anti-Saloon League did all that it could to criminalize homebrewing, but it would take until 1925 before it was able to get it banned.[142]

There were other success stories during Prohibition, one of them even involving legally selling alcohol. Even during Prohibition, alcohol was not necessarily illegal to sell, provided the customer had a doctor's prescription. One of the favorite treatments was a product called Peruna, a patent medicine developed by noted Columbus doctor Samuel Hartman. According to Hartman, his tonic was the cure to just about every ailment; the recipe, he said, was given to him in a dream by the ghost of an Indian chief.[143] Perhaps not the most believable story, but Peruna proved to be massively popular in the 1880s, due in no small part to its 27 percent alcohol content.[144] With the funds generated from Peruna, Hartman was able to build the Hartman Hotel, the Hartman Theatre and the Hartman Farm, which at the time was among the largest farms east of the Mississippi.[145]

Hartman Farm. *Courtesy of the Library of Congress.*

Hartman Theatre. *Courtesy of the Library of Congress.*

For decades, Peruna generated a massive fortune for Dr. Hartman, but fortune could change swiftly. In 1906, Hartman was forced to reduce the alcohol content of Peruna due to the Pure Food and Drug Act. Needless to say, sales plunged. Hartman died the year before Prohibition took effect, but it probably would have heartened him to see Peruna thriving again. Although it no longer had more than 20 percent alcohol, Peruna could be legally obtained, and it still had a kick over twice that of wine.[146]

There were other ways to be successful during Prohibition, although these ways involved shirking the law. All legal saloons closed on May 27, 1919, but it would be foolish to think that drinking actually stopped.

CHAPTER 8

PROHIBITION AND THE ANTI-SALOON LEAGUE

The ratification of the Eighteenth Amendment would seem to be the end of the story for the Anti-Saloon League. Its fight would seem to be over after Prohibition became enshrined in the Constitution. Victory, however, would not be kind. Now that Prohibition was in effect, what need was there for an organization that owed its existence to fighting against the saloon? That was the question that now faced the Anti-Saloon League. It would soon become apparent that its fight was not actually over—it just got a bit more complicated.

At the beginning of Prohibition, the Anti-Saloon League was the most powerful lobbying group in the nation; by the time the Twentieth Amendment was passed, it was in shambles. What happened? The leadership of the Anti-Saloon League was aware of the fact that just because alcohol was illegal to sell, it did not mean that people would actually stop drinking it. Leadership of the Anti-Saloon League would fracture, though, when it came to figuring out what to do about this. One camp, led by Ernest Cherrington, held the belief that education was the key to making sure that Prohibition was effective. The other faction, led by Wayne Wheeler, promoted strict enforcement of the law to strong-arm people into being obedient to Prohibition. The story of the Anti-Saloon League during Prohibition was shaped by its infighting. The tension and hostility between the Cherrington and Wheeler wings of the Anti-Saloon League created an existential crisis over just what the league should be.

The rift in the Anti-Saloon League began early in Prohibition but took time to grow into a crisis. From the very beginning, the league faced a crisis of a different kind: funding. Astutely noted by Ernest Cherrington, "The greatest danger which today threatens the Prohibition movement in American and throughout the world, is that in this hour of victory the faithful friends of prohibition may conclude that the fight against the liquor traffic in America is at an end."[147] Cherrington was worried that because the Eighteenth Amendment passed, all of those who had supported the league in its fight would stop donating. This was a legitimate concern on Cherrington's part and one that would plague the league throughout the entirety of Prohibition.

Cherrington and Wheeler's sparring within the Anti-Saloon League distracted the league from its mission, but it was the lack of funding that would keep it from being able to effectively act on either's plans. It was true that after Prohibition passed, the Anti-Saloon League did lose many of its former supporters. Churches stopped participating in local leagues, and funders did not see the point in further support. They had won, hadn't they? At the very moment of victory, the Anti-Saloon League was potentially mortally wounded.[148] The sudden lack of funds and the growing rift between Cherrington and Wheeler hollowed out the Anti-Saloon League—as soon as Prohibition became law, there was no one capable of defending dry interests.

The league put on a brave public front and, for a while, managed to keep its internal turmoil hidden from view. A lack of funds, however, meant that the Anti-Saloon League was not able to fuel its propaganda machine as well as it had before. Wayne Wheeler wanted to make a law enforcement handbook that included all the different temperance laws from all the states. It was supposed to be a guidebook for local law enforcement officers to use so that they were aware of what laws applied in their jurisdictions.[149] The handbook was a noble goal and would have been a useful tool for understanding the confusing world of Prohibition. It was never published, though, as funds could not be found. Ernest Cherrington's camp also experienced firsthand the problems that arise when the purse strings begin to tighten. Publication of the *American Issue* became rather erratic, and supplemental materials were never produced.[150] No supporters meant no money, and no money meant that they could not engender the public's support like they used to. The league was able to do little to solve this predicament because the leadership was soon deeply involved in a civil war between the education and the enforcement wings.

The story of the Anti-Saloon League during Prohibition is that of these two men, Ernest Cherrington and Wayne Wheeler. Both men held high positions within the ranks of the league. Based in Westerville was Cherrington, the general editor of the *American Issue* and superintendent of the finance department of the league. In Washington, D.C., Wheeler was the league's legislative superintendent. Both men had impressive credentials to their names by the time of the passage of the Eighteenth Amendment. Cherrington was at the helm of one of the world's most powerful and well-oiled propaganda machines and had revolutionized the financial structure of the league. By 1919, Purley Baker, the Anti-Saloon League's general superintendent, was living in semi-retirement in New Mexico, leaving Cherrington as the de facto leader at the league headquarters in Westerville.[151]

Now that national Prohibition had been achieved, Cherrington saw that the key to ensuring its success was through education. This stance was not a new development, as Cherrington had been unwavering in his belief in the power of education all along. "The requirements of national dry strategy were thus first and foremost education," he had said.[152] During the fight to pass the national amendment, Cherrington summed up his view of how Prohibition would work: "Prohibition would eventuate only after an ever larger portion of Americans were persuaded that it was a wise policy for them personally, for their state and nation, and eventually for mankind. Moreover winning dry laws helped with education work, just as the reverse was true. As more and more citizens witnessed the social benefits of prohibition firsthand, they would agree to obey the low as well as seek it."[153]

As far back as 1911, Cherrington foresaw the type of divisions that now faced the league, claiming that "it was of little use to enact prohibition laws in places where public sentiment made enforcement unlikely."[154] Cherrington held fast to his belief that the "[Eighteenth Amendment's] objective was not to make men good, but to protect society" and that "legislation and enforcement...cannot alone solve the beverage alcohol problem. That can be done only as enlightened public opinion is translated into law and conduct."[155]

Wheeler was the man who was primarily responsible for the political successes of the league. Wheeler had almost the exact opposite opinion of enforcement and education. For Wheeler, the purpose of education was just to teach obedience to the law.[156] Education was not a means of creating an enlightened population that would willingly decide to reject alcohol but rather a means to let people know the risks of *not* following the law. Wheeler did not think particularly highly of Cherrington's focus on education or of his vision of a self-policing population. According to Wheeler, "The league was strictly a political organization, not some transcendent temperance education movement against the kingdom of evil."[157]

Perhaps Wheeler did not find Cherrington's methods to be practical, or maybe he saw him as a threat to his own power. Wheeler wanted to fashion himself into a "dry boss," a sort of power broker who could control every aspect of Prohibition from dispensing of patronage to candidates facing election to drafting the laws. It was Wheeler who would select candidates to be endorsed by the league and put pressure on senators and congressmen, causing them to support the dry goals of the Anti-Saloon League. Without Wayne Wheeler's efforts in the nation's capital, the Anti-Saloon League would never have been such a strong political force. Wheeler's personal secretary claimed that he "controlled six congresses, dictated to two presidents of the United States, directed legislation in most of the States of the Union, picked the candidates for the more important elective state and federal offices, held the balance of power in both Republican and Democratic parties, distributed more patronage than any dozen other men, supervised a federal bureau from outside without official authority, and was recognized by friend and foe alike as the most masterful and powerful single individual in the United States."[158]

Perhaps it was the power that Wheeler wielded in Washington that shaped his belief that Prohibition could only succeed through coercive law enforcement methods. Wheeler could not be bothered to try to convince people that Prohibition was for their own good—the law should be enough. Speaking on the possibility that Prohibition would be difficult to control, Wheeler was quoted as saying, "If there is any part of this nation that is so lacking in patriotism that it will defy the law the federal government must provide the power to enforce the law."[159] The attack on patriotism was a favorite tactic for Wheeler. In 1920, he had made similar comments: "[A]ny state which is so lacking in loyalty and patriotism that it will not enact appropriate legislation to enforce the 18th Amendment must be made to obey the laws of the united states. Loyalty to the Constitution means the enactment and enforcement of effective prohibition laws."[160]

Even though the league was badly wounded, it did not mean that it was not able to do anything during Prohibition. Both wings of the Anti-Saloon League did have their own projects and goals.

Both Cherrington and Wheeler believed that the Anti-Saloon League had done the world a great service by getting the Eighteenth Amendment passed; both also had the desire to do what they saw as the natural extension of that work. Cherrington had lofty, and unrealistic, goals for Prohibition. National Prohibition was a good first step, but the rest of the world was still suffering under the reign of the liquor traffic. It was Cherrington's goal to create a world where no one would be drinking alcohol at all.

Beginning even before the ratification of the Eighteenth Amendment, Cherrington initiated plans for what would be the World League Against Alcoholism. Officially founded at the 1919 convention of the Anti-Saloon League, the World League Against Alcoholism was born with delegates from numerous countries, including the United States, Canada, Mexico, Japan, Scotland, Ireland, England, France, Belgium, Denmark, Switzerland, New Zealand, Sweden, Czechoslovakia and Italy.[161] The new organization's mission was to "go attain by the means of education and legislation, the total suppression throughout the world of Alcoholism which is the poisoning of the body....This League pledges itself to avoid affiliation with any political party as such, and to maintain an attitude of strict neutrality in all questions of public policy, not directly and immediately concerned with the traffic of alcoholic beverages."[162]

The mission reflects the personal view of Cherrington, in that it distinctly gives education a primary role over law enforcement in its means of combating the alcohol problem. The World League Against Alcoholism was a widely ambitious undertaking, especially since national Prohibition had only just begun. In some ways, the World League does appear to be the "transcendent temperance education movement against the kingdom of evil"[163] that Wheeler railed against. Such an undertaking does seem more like tilting at windmills rather than a serious attempt to bring an end to drinking, especially in light of the fact that the Anti-Saloon League itself was having trouble raising the necessary funds it needed to stay afloat. Given that at one point in 1921, Cherrington was even forced to sell the paper stockpiles for the *American Issue* to fund the Anti-Saloon League, there was simply no way he could raise the money for an even larger organization.[164]

In actuality, the World League Against Alcoholism was only ever able to field one branch office, in London, which only had one employee.[165] Prohibition was a frustrating time for the editor of the *American Issue*. At almost every turn, Cherrington was stifled. His grand scheme to bring about world Prohibition was never able to truly get off the ground, and as the finance director for the Anti-Saloon League, he was constantly faced with the problems of keeping the league fiscally solvent. Later, in 1925, Cherrington was passed over for the general superintendent position in the National Anti-Saloon League position due to underhanded attacks by the Wheeler wing.

Wayne Wheeler had a different set of priorities for the Anti-Saloon League during Prohibition. The first priority was to be able to defeat any attack on national Prohibition. Wheeler knew that just because Prohibition was law now, it did not mean that it always would be. To ensure that it stayed on the books, the Anti-Saloon League would need to continue to promote dry candidates for legislative positions. The second step was to prohibit Americans from engaging in liquor traffic with other counties. National Prohibition would be next to useless if there were still ways to get alcohol, Wheeler reasoned. Wheeler's third priority was to go after the use of peyote, perhaps because he believed that in lieu of alcohol people would go looking for substitutes. The fourth of Wheeler's priorities was to pass legislation for the nationalization of liquor stocks.[166] Under the Eighteenth Amendment, it was legal to possess alcohol—just not to sell it or drink it. Wheeler saw the fact that many of the liquor producers were sitting on large stockpiles as a deeply troubling situation. He believed—probably correctly, in some cases—that these stockpiles would trickle illicitly into the possession of the public, thus undermining the national Prohibition amendment. The matter of liquor stockpiles had actually long been a concern of the Anti-Saloon League. The league's idea was for all alcohol to be redistilled into industrial ethyl alcohol, which would, or at least should, destroy its uses for drinking.[167] Although in some ways Wheeler's actions may have been a bit self-serving, they could at least be argued as being a little more realistic than Cherrington's.

Wheeler believed that with Prohibition as law, it was necessary for there to be a way to make sure that it was followed. It is a sign of just how powerful Wheeler was that he, an unelected individual, was the one who originally drafted the bill, nicknamed the Volstead Act after its sponsor, that governed how to enforce Prohibition. Wheeler was a frequent guest on Capitol Hill, where he often testified before the Senate Judiciary Subcommittee arguing for expanded law enforcement methods for Prohibition. Among Wheeler's ideas were expanding search warrants and limiting the amount of alcohol private citizens were able to keep "so as to prevent homes from becoming speakeasies."[168] The idea that private homes would become speakeasies was a constant source of concern for Wheeler and one that was actually a legitimate issue.

When the National Prohibition Act, or the Volstead Act, was passed, Wheeler was able to achieve some successes: he successfully talked Congress into keeping the limit of alcohol in beer to 0.5 percent by arguing that 2.3 percent beer was still intoxicating and people would simply drink it in proportionally larger quantities.[169] Even now we can begin to see how Wheeler's ego might be beginning to get the best of him. Shortly after the passage of the Volstead Act, Wheeler called on the various local branches of the Anti-Saloon League to monitor law enforcement officers to see if they were following the new laws and report violations back to him.[170] The clash of egos between Cherrington and Wheeler would soon begin to tear the league apart at the seams, but for now, let's leave the organization for a while. There was much more going on in Columbus while the Anti-Saloon League began its road toward civil war.

Chapter 9

SPEAKEASIES

Wwe switch gears from reporting on those who did not drink to telling the story of those who did. Even though it was falling apart, the Anti-Saloon League tried to put on a strong front and did manage to keep publishing material aimed at convincing everyone that the story of Prohibition was one of a happy, law-abiding citizenry and a place where all saloons were closed and no one drank alcohol. Was its position true? Of course not. What makes the story of Prohibition intriguing is those who flaunted the law and drank anyway.

Prohibition was a trying time for those who enjoyed to drink, at least if you did not know where to look. Columbus, like most large cities, had its less than reputable side. By some accounts, "Columbus had 100 speakeasies and Beer flats and approximately 4000 bootleggers. Hotel attendants specialize in quick service and provide fairly good liquor too."[171] The saloon did not go away; it merely went underground. Speakeasies in Columbus were not as prevalent as they might have been in other cities, although due to their illicit nature it is impossible to get an exact number. Certainly, running a speakeasy could be a profitable venture. At least at the beginning of Prohibition, it was not necessarily a venture that was all that risky either. The penalties for selling alcohol were minor. The fines were so small compared to the profits that could be made from selling illegal alcohol that there was no real incentive to stop even if you did get caught. This was actually a problem that all of the Anti-Saloon League could agree on, and Wayne Wheeler spoke to the Senate Judiciary Committee to try to convince the body to draft stricter

The soda fountain. *Courtesy of the Library of Congress.*

laws regarding bootlegging and limiting the amount people could keep in their own homes "so as to prevent homes from becoming speakeasies."[172]

Of course, individuals did sell illegal alcohol out of their homes, but there were also a number of saloons that never completely got out of the alcohol business. The shining example of how a speakeasy could hide in plain sight behind legitimate businesses was Bott Bros. Located in downtown Columbus, Bott Bros. had been one of the premier saloons in the city; its bar had even won a blue ribbon for craftsmanship at the 1893 Columbia Exposition in Chicago.[173] The transition of Bott Bros. from a saloon into a soda fountain was actually covered by the *Columbus Dispatch*. The *Dispatch* recorded how "the present staff will continue to serve plain and fancy drinks of the soft variety."[174] At the time, it was heralded as an example of how former saloons could make the transition work. There was only one problem with the accolades: it has been rumored that Bott Bros. was actually a speakeasy.[175] This would put an interesting spin on the stories in the *Dispatch*. Instead of being a beacon of the success of transition to "legitimate business," all the changes that were made could be viewed as a front projecting an aura of respectability. Many of the other rumored speakeasies were located in what is now known as German Village, which is directly to the east of the Brewery District. That does not mean all speakeasies were within walking distance of the former breweries.

One speakeasy in the neighborhood of Clintonville, a few miles north of downtown on High Street, was located in a private residence that had been made out of a church that had been a stop on the Underground Railroad.[176]

Confiscated liquor being disposed of. *Courtesy of the Library of Congress.*

Near the heart of downtown Columbus, there is a tiny little restaurant called the Ringside Café. In the days before Prohibition, it was named the Chamber of Commerce Café, and when it became apparent that Prohibition was coming, the Columbus Chamber of Commerce sensed which way the wind was blowing. Not wanting to be associated with a place that served alcohol, it pushed to get the name changed.[177] It was probably just as wise that it did—although operating during Prohibition under the moniker the Jolly Gargoyle, the establishment was still probably selling alcohol.[178]

Closer to the former breweries, in German Village, was the building that now is home to the Old Mohawk. Although only suspected of having housed a speakeasy in the back of the grocery store in the building, there is a legend about a visit there from none other than legendary gangster Al Capone.[179] There have been very few conclusively documented speakeasies in Columbus, for the obvious reasons that their owners wished their establishments to remain clandestine. One true speakeasy is now known as the Hey Hey Bar, which prior to Prohibition had been a saloon owned by August Wagner.[180] The current name of the bar, in fact, comes from the illicit Prohibition activities. During Prohibition, the building officially became a grocery store, which we know was sometimes a sign that illegal activities could be going on inside. In the back, there was a clandestine speakeasy. Bootleggers would knock on the back door and give a call of "Hey hey, the beer is here," alerting the owners about their illegal product.[181]

Chapter 10

THE BREWERS AND THE BREWERY DISTRICT

We have seen how the Columbus brewers played a large role in shaping their neighborhood and, to a degree, the entire South End of town. After losing the battle with the Anti-Saloon League, the brewers were facing—by coincidence much like the league—an existential crisis about how to proceed in the future. Prohibition was an unwelcome guest on Columbus's South End. It wreaked havoc with the breweries and put many hardworking people out of their jobs. This loss in jobs for the breweries would eventually lead to an exodus from the Brewery District, which left it to decay for decades.

Where the Anti-Saloon League seemed to flail about trying to figure out its place in Prohibition, the brewers were acutely aware of the fact that the law would change their lives. Prohibition for the brewers meant that their livelihoods were under attack—every township, every county and every state that voted to go dry was a blow against the brewers.

Given that the brewing companies saw Prohibition coming years in advance, most of them started to make preparations ahead of time. This, of course, did not mean that they were all successful; most were not. By the end of Prohibition, only one brewery in the Brewery District was still in business. The law did not immediately put the breweries out of business, as most of them tried to make a go of it. This part of the story is how the Columbus brewers tried to continue in a world where their former jobs were illegal. One way was to stay in a business the breweries were uniquely prepared for: they could actually still make beer. Hoping that their customers liked their products for more than just alcohol, making near beer was a popular choice of the brewers. The Hoster Columbus Company began making its cereal beverage Bruin back in 1917 to drum up a loyal customer base for the inevitable time when Prohibition became a reality. Nearly all of the now former breweries made an attempt to outlast Prohibition by making cereal beverages. Along with Hoster Columbus, the August Wagner and Sons Products Company, as August Wagner's business was now known after he took full control of the Gambrinus, also made a cereal beverage, as did the Franklin Brewing Company, the Ohio Beverage Company (formerly the Ohio Brewing Company) and the Washington Company (formerly Washington Brewing Company).[182]

Making a cereal beverage was all well and good, but most of the former brewing companies were not naïve enough to believe that simply making non-alcoholic beer would be enough to keep them in business. There were two options that the brewers identified as ways to try to keep their businesses open. One option was simply to make something else. There was nothing that precluded products other than beer from being made at the former breweries, and with their facilities going unused for alcoholic beverage production, the breweries had just the infrastructure needed for making soft drinks or ice.

Some of the breweries did not anticipate disaster with Prohibition and even believed that it created new opportunities. The day after Prohibition began, the *Columbus Dispatch* ran an article detailing the brewers' future plans. Hoster Columbus would make Bruin and a few other soft drinks, including Gold Top Ginger Ale, hoping that it could capitalize on the old Gold Top name. Hoster did, though, have to lay off a number of employees in anticipation of lower sales than it had been experiencing. Other brewers actually displayed a fair amount of optimism. The Ohio Beverage Company owners were so optimistic, or delusional, about their chances during Prohibition that when the other breweries were tightening their belts, they actually hired new staff.[183] The Ohio Beverage Company produced soft drinks, including their cereal beverage Cold Seal, as well as Whistle, Swetts root beer and Ohio Club ginger ale.[184]

It might not be immediately obvious, but there was a difference between what Hoster and the Ohio Beverage Company did. The soft drinks that Hoster Columbus was making were products created by Hoster; Gold Top was Hoster's own line of ginger ale. This was not the case with the Ohio Beverage Company. While it did create its own cereal beverage, Cold Seal, it decided that rather than create its own line of unknown soft drinks to try

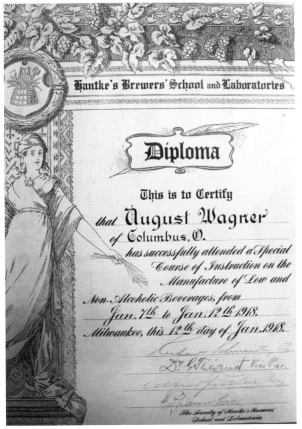

Above: Champagne Mist was one of the soft drinks made by Hoster Columbus. *Courtesy of the German Village Society.*

Left: August Wagner's license allowing him to produce cereal beverages. *Courtesy of the German Village Society.*

to compete with established brands, the Ohio Beverage Company simply allowed its facilities to be used for the production of existing drinks from existing companies. Whistle is, in fact, still around today. The Ohio Beverage Company had the facilities for production, so it turned itself into a regional producer of other products. Later, the Ohio Beverage Company became the Wyandot Soda Company to try to sell soft drinks under a name unaffiliated with its alcoholic past.[185]

August Wagner's first act during Prohibition was to buy complete control of the Gambrinus Brewing Company and change the name to the August Wagner and Sons Products Company, under which he produced a line of his own soft drinks and cereal beverages. The second thing that Wagner did was buy up former saloon properties through one of his other businesses, the August Wagner Realty Company.[186] Saloons, particularly those that had been downtown and the areas surrounding it, had been particularly desirable locations. By purchasing the former saloon properties, Wagner gained some of the most valuable land in downtown Columbus. Even Prohibition did not stop Wagner from making alcohol anyway. One of the many products produced by the August Wagner and Sons Products Company was a malt tonic that was sold as a medicine.[187] This was probably a particularly profitable move, as by Prohibition Wagner had a significant amount of name recognition in Columbus, and we have seen what making medicine did for Peruna.

The brewers knew that Prohibition was coming and had been preparing for it for a number of years. Trade papers were full of stories about what the various breweries were going to do about Prohibition now that it was the law. The *Western Brewer and Journal*'s September 1919 edition follows up on the Columbus brewers. The Franklin Brewery, which refused to comment to the *Dispatch*, settled on making a cereal beverage and an orange drink. In addition to the drinks Hoster told the *Dispatch* it was going to make, it also decided to use its refrigeration facilities for storage and making ice. The Washington Brewing Company became the Washington Company and settled on making a cereal beverage. The Ohio Beverage Company did actually see an increase in sales during the first few months of Prohibition. This might have been an indication that either it was not that successful when it made beer or it had just prepared for Prohibition better than the others. Sales increased so much for the Ohio Beverage Company that in addition to adding staff, it also purchased new bottling machinery.[188]

August Wagner took control of Gambrinus and proceeded to make "cereal beverages and soft drinks on an extensive scale."[189] Wagner's cereal

CONTENTS 12 FLUID OZ.

PERMIT OHIO L-1

AWARDED
BADGE OF HONOR
MEDAL AND DIPLOMA
ANTWERP, BELGIUM

AWARDED
CROSS OF HONOR
MEDAL AND DIPLOMA
PARIS, FRANCE.

ALCOHOLIC CONTENT LESS THAN ½ OF 1% BY VOLUME

AUGUSTINER

MADE AND BOTTLED EXCLUSIVELY BY
THE AUGUST WAGNER & SONS PRODUCTS CO.
COLUMBUS, OHIO.

Wagner made a cereal beverage version of Augustiner during Prohibition. *Courtesy of the German Village Society.*

beverage was simply a version of its award-wining Augustiner beer with reduced alcohol. To reassure the customers, ads from the August Wagner and Sons Products Company during Prohibition proclaimed that the new Augustiner tasted the same as the old version.[190] Of course, despite all their preparations, Prohibition was unkind to the Columbus brewers. We know how this ended for the brewers—despite their best intentions, most of them would not still be in business by the time Prohibition ended in 1933. It seemed that the market for cereal beverages and other soft drinks was simply not large enough.

One of the first casualties of Prohibition was none other than the Louis Hoster Company. In 1924, nearly one hundred years after Hoster opened his brewery, the Hoster Columbus Company went out of business. Hoster products did not immediately disappear from the market, though, as many of the company's assets were purchased by its former brewmaster, August Wagner.[191] Under August Wagner, Gold Top Ginger Ale and Hoster's grape-flavored soft drink, Champagne Mist, were still being made. The year 1924 also spelled the end for the Washington Company following a raid by federal Prohibition agents.[192]

Select label. *Courtesy of the German Village Society.*

It is safe to say that Columbus going dry was not a positive experience for the neighborhood now known as the Brewery District. The breweries were the anchor of the neighborhood, as many of their workers lived in the surrounding neighborhood. It should be remembered that these workers were better paid than those who worked in other businesses.[193] Temperance agitators did not seem to realize, or care, that there were plenty of hardworking individuals who would be faced with losing their jobs once their plans for national Prohibition took effect.

As the Anti-Saloon League ramped up its attacks on the brewing industry, the brewers were increasingly faced with tough choices to make. In order to keep their businesses operating, the breweries had to find ways to cut costs. A common method to cut costs was to shed underperforming aspects of the company. We know how the Hoster Columbus breweries closed down various breweries over the years. These closures meant that the Hoster Columbus Company was able to stay in business, but they also meant that many workers suddenly found themselves without jobs.

The closing of the plants had a tremendous impact on the Brewery District neighborhood. Even before Prohibition actually started, workers were beginning to lose their jobs. Without their jobs to tie them to the neighborhood, many of the former brewery workers were forced to leave in search of new jobs elsewhere. As Prohibition wore on and more of the

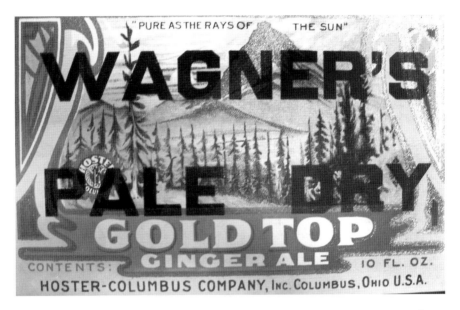

Gold Top continued to be made by August Wagner after Hoster Columbus went out of business. *Courtesy of the German Village Society.*

former breweries were shuttered, it became increasingly clear to the former employees that their jobs were not going to be coming back soon. The closing breweries set off a chain reaction that left the Brewery District nearly vacant for more than fifty years. Breweries closing meant that brewery workers were no longer employed, which meant that they no longer had income to spend; this, in turn, drove out the businesses that catered to the workers. Without people working at the breweries, the people who made uniforms for the brewery workers could not make money or afford to go to restaurants, and the list goes on.[194]

By the end of Prohibition, the Brewery District was close to being abandoned.[195] Looking at the Brewery District toward the end of Prohibition, one can see the results of the Anti-Saloon League's scorched-earth attacks on the brewing industry. There were few jobs left for the few people who remained there. The exodus from the Brewery District was devastating to the South End and set it up for years of decline and demolition.[196]

CHAPTER **11**

BOOTLEGGERS, COP KILLERS AND CORRUPTION

The word *Prohibition* often conjures up images of mobsters with Tommy guns and high-speed police chases. It is safe to say that the story of Prohibition in Columbus does not really feature either of those. In contrast to larger cities such as Chicago, Columbus's story was rather tame when it came to crime during Prohibition. Not that illicit activities did not take place in Columbus. They did, but they were just not as dramatic as elsewhere. Major crimes during Prohibition, such as bootleggers murdering people, were rare and widely documented. Other lesser crimes, such as homebrewing, small-scale bootlegging or smuggling, were more difficult to uncover, so it is unknown how much these actually happened. Of course, these things did happen, and the newspapers were full of stories when they came to light. What is amazing is just how naïve the Anti-Saloon League and even senior law enforcement officials were about the impact Prohibition would have on crime. It certainly seemed that the Anti-Saloon League actually believed that most of the crime in this country was due to alcohol, as if people who did not drink were incapable of breaking the law.

Every Prohibition story has to have its mobsters. Let's get Columbus's mob story out of the way. It is not so much a story about mobsters in Columbus but of how they were kept *out*. Much of the story is in the realm of legend, and it is unverifiable. But something did have to happen to keep the mob out. Columbus's story features none other than the most famous of all gangsters, Al Capone. The story goes that during Prohibition, Capone was interested in opening up bootlegging operations in Columbus, but for some reason,

Prohibition agents. *Courtesy of the Library of Congress.*

he was convinced not to. Capone did, in fact, visit Columbus; that is not in question. What exactly happened during the visit is, however. One rumor was that Capone visited German Village to scout the Old Mohawk, which was supposedly a speakeasy at the time. The legend goes that Capone met with a man by the name of Pat Murnan, who convinced him that he should not extend his operations into Columbus.[197] Whether or not the meeting actually took place, Capone did decide to not open up operations in Columbus.

As the man who might have kept the Chicago mob out of Columbus, Murnan deserves a mention in our story. A larger-than-life character in

Columbus history, Murnan often dressed in loud colors and patterned suits and carried around a cane with a gold handle. His common-law wife was the madam of a brothel near his taxi business.[198] He had many occupations throughout his life in Columbus, including running a taxi company, but it was for his gambling operations that he was primarily known. His gambling den was "above Doersam's Restaurant at 13½ West Broad Street, near to which he often had some of his taxis parked for built-in business."[199] Later in his life, Murnan once claimed that his job was to "accept wagers on the speed and endurances of thoroughbred horses."[200] In his obituary, Murnan was hailed as a "Gentleman Sports man and philanthropist and one of Columbus most beloved figures."[201] He was notably generous and on some level cared very much for the well-being of his city, having donated to a variety of causes. He was once credited as saying that "a man only needs so much money and if he makes any more he should give it to charity." Although not definitive proof of his meeting with Capone, Murnan's obituary stated that he employed "methods [that] were bulwark against the influx of undesirables into Columbus and [was a] valuable ally of the police against racketeering [and was] frequently acknowledged for his service for keeping Columbus clean of many of the evils that infect other cities."[202] This could have perhaps been a reference to the legend that he had met with Capone and kept out-of-state bootleggers from taking over the city. As for the exact methods he employed to keep Columbus clean, these are never mentioned.

What sort of crime was Columbus faced with during Prohibition, and how much? That all depends on who you happen to ask. The story of crime during Prohibition is murky. Certain forces, such as the Anti-Saloon League, had every reason to downplay the amount of crime. One of the major selling points for national Prohibition from the league was a promised reduction in crime. According to the league, of course, crime had dropped off during Prohibition. Every year, the Anti-Saloon League published a *Yearbook*, updating readers on how well Prohibition was working. Harry Davis, governor of Ohio, testified that the "view sometimes heard that crime has been increased by Prohibition is erroneous in [his] opinion." He did, however, hedge this by noting that if there was an increase in crime, it would be because there was not adequate enforcement of the new laws, a view that would have been in line with the beliefs of Wayne Wheeler.[203] Columbus mayor James Thomas claimed that "it is very rare to see a person on the streets under the influence of intoxicants."[204] The mayor's suggestion did actually have some evidence to back it up. The *Columbus Dispatch* reported that during the second full month of Prohibition, there were just 32 arrests for public drunkenness, down from 155 the year before, a decrease of almost 80 percent.[205]

Columbus police chief H.E. French also sang the praises of Prohibition, saying that "men who had been drunkards secured positions and became good citizens. Assault and Battery cases and other misdemeanors of like character were reduced to a minimum and upon one occasion the Police department of this city did not make a single arrest for over 24 hours."[206] Chief French also hedged his statement by adding that "at this time we were very optimistic because crime conditions were also reduced to a minimum and this happy condition obtained until the government began to issue removal and transportation permits and almost immediately the bootlegger became a real problem and we have been waging a warfare with this class of offenders ever since."[207] This was kind of a strange testimonial for the Anti-Saloon League to publish, as it seemed to say both that there was almost no crime and that it was a real problem.

Crime during Prohibition was obviously a concern from the beginning. The Anti-Saloon League was deeply worried about speakeasies and bootlegging. Chief French was concerned that the people committing crimes were *not* drinking now. Perhaps this might seem like a strange thing to be concerned about, but Chief French's duties extended beyond Prohibition enforcement, and he was worried about crimes being committed that were not necessarily related to Prohibition. He was actually worried that, to some degree, the fact that alcohol was illegal would make it harder for his force to do their jobs. Shortly after Prohibition began, Chief French issued a statement to his force: "In the days before Prohibition, it was common…for criminals to drink freely before committing a crime. Usually some mistake was made during the crime, or some inadvertent act done afterwards that made apprehension relatively easy."[208] His argument was that because they were no longer drunks, criminals were getting smarter, and so, too, must be the law enforcement officers. This was not exactly a glowing recommendation for the Columbus police force, that they were apparently only intelligent enough to catch criminals who were inebriated. Frequently, the criminals during Prohibition were still drinking anyway, so his concern was really moot. Chief French would have known that his speech was not true from the beginning. Not even a month after Columbus went dry, four people were arrested for public drunkenness by Town and Front Streets, close to the heart of downtown. Those arrested were interrogated by Chief French himself.[209]

No, public drunkenness did not stop. Sometimes those arrested tried to lie about their reasons. Harry Feasel was arrested for drinking whiskey only to claim that it was for hay fever; he earned a jail sentence of fifteen days. Others were unabashed about their reasons for drinking. Rebecca Simmons's "only excuse was being dry." Her honesty earned her thirty days in the workhouse.[210] Aside from public drunkenness, bootlegging appears to have been the most common Prohibition violation in Columbus. For those who wanted a drink with a kick, finding someone to buy it from was apparently not a difficult proposition. Famed Columbus artist Leland McClelland was a student at The Ohio State University toward the end of Prohibition and recalled how "it was possible to get a quart of beer from 25 cents from a bootlegger…and it was high-powered stuff."[211]

Undoubtedly, there was a fair amount of bootlegging going on in Columbus. The Anti-Saloon League's concern with homebrewing was not unfounded. It is likely that much of the bootleg alcohol in Columbus was done on a very small scale by homebrewers, often for their own use or in small distributions. Larger operations, though, did frequently involve importing alcohol from outside the city. In many ways, bootlegging is proof that Cherrington's education approach to the alcohol problem was not entirely successful.

The Anti-Saloon League had been bombarding people with propaganda for almost thirty years by the time Prohibition was ratified, and there was little chance that the bootleggers had not encountered some of the literature at some point. In this case, Wayne Wheeler did seem to have the correct point of view. Wheeler had long been concerned that penalties for violating Prohibition laws were not strict enough.[212] The financial benefits from continuing to bootleg far exceeded the meager fines that were incurred for doing it, so there was absolutely no incentive to end bootlegging. At the beginning of Prohibition, there was even some confusion as to who exactly was supposed to be doing the enforcement. The inspectors from the Liquor Licensing Agency were not working as enforcers because the Ohio attorney general claimed that the agency stopped existing when Prohibition went into effect.[213] It would take the Supreme Court to decide if the inspectors did, in fact, lose their jobs.[214] The offices for the Prohibition Commission would open in January 1920.[215]

From the beginning of Prohibition, the *Columbus Dispatch* frequently ran stories about the various Prohibition-related crimes that were occurring, however minor they might have been. From these stories, one can piece together the different types of alcohol-related crime Columbus was experiencing. Such stories ran from the very minor, such as that of John Shirly, who was driving his taxi drunk and snapped a telephone pole, to that of the murder committed by Columbus city treasurer Elmer Jenkins.[216]

Early stories give little evidence of any sort of connection between any of the crimes. They mostly seem to tell the stories of isolated incidents. From these, it is clear that drinking certainly did not stop, and because of this, neither did making alcohol or transporting it. Since the breweries and distilleries could not make their product any longer, at least not legally, alcohol suddenly became much more scarce. The demand for it was certainly not lessened. There were some who probably did stop drinking because of Prohibition, but there were many individuals who would not. These people needed to get their liquor somewhere.

There were many ways for enterprising individuals to procure alcohol. One was simply to steal it. Stories in the newspapers within just a month of Prohibition's passage recorded how thieves would break into homes to rob the cellars of stored liquor. It appears that after only a short period of time, there was already such a shortage of liquor that people needed to resort to thievery to get their fix.[217] Stealing alcohol seemed to have actually been a fairly common tactic for obtaining liquor. In January 1920, C.T Hughes reported eleven cases of liquor with a value of $775 stolen from his home.[218] Theft was not only limited to common criminals. It appears that police officers, those very individuals charged with the enforcement of Prohibition, were also, from time to time, taking part in stealing alcohol. Joe Saunders was arrested for bootlegging out of his home, and twenty-four half-pint bottles were taken as evidence. By the next Monday, the evidence had disappeared from the prison even though "[t]he entire force of turnkeys at the city prison deny letting the liquor get away."[219]

It seems that early on in Prohibition, Columbus dried up pretty fast. National Prohibition did not go into effect until January 1920, which meant that if you wanted to have alcohol in Columbus after May 1919, all you had to do was bring it in from outside. Bringing outside liquor into Columbus began almost as soon as Prohibition did. One of the first cases was that of William Sample and Edward Wittmeyer of Columbus, who crashed their car in Bowling Green while driving under the influence. Wittmeyer fractured his ribs, and Sample's wooden leg was splinted. Their car was carrying two hundred quarts and three hundred sample bottles of whiskey that were being taken from Toledo to Columbus. Had it not been for the fact that those two appeared to be enjoying their wares while driving, all of that liquor could have made it to the streets of Columbus.

By 1925, the amounts of incoming liquor got larger, and train cars were needed to ship it into Columbus. That year, 270 gallons of alcohol were seized from George Huff, including liquor from a train car at the Pennsylvania rail station. This trainload was part of a larger bootlegging ring that was shipping alcohol from Philadelphia to Columbus.[220] Just as officials in charge of enforcing the law were not above the theft of liquor, they were also not above being party to its transportation. In 1925, it was discovered, embarrassingly, that the State Welfare garage in downtown Columbus was being used as a "rendezvous for bootleggers and a distribution center for their wares." It was further discovered that trustees from the Mansfield Reformatory were working with the bootleggers. When the garage was raided, a car containing 60-gallon cans of moonshine was confiscated. The trustees were arrested and sentenced to time for burglary and larceny.[221]

Despite Prohibition laws, individuals went to surprising lengths to ensure that there was available alcohol. There were other cases of corruption in Columbus during Prohibition. In 1925, Columbus businessman Lawrence Riehl was arrested for conspiracy and bribery.[222] It turned out that in addition to being a successful Columbus businessman, Riehl was also part of an interstate bootlegging operation. In 1924, a few bootleggers had been captured and were in the state penitentiary in Atlanta, Georgia. Riehl was paid $10,500 by one of the bootleggers, Willie Haar, to procure "special privileges" for his captured relatives.[223] Riehl ended up traveling to Georgia to meet with prison chaplain T.P. Hayden in order to buy his allegiance to the plan to obtain the "special privileges."[224] In the end, Riehl and Albert Sartain, the warden at the penitentiary, were convicted and sentenced to a year in prison.[225]

Rather than buy their liquor from others, some individuals tried their hands at making their own. Perhaps it was cheaper to make your own liquor, but that did not mean it always worked out. In September 1919, there were many arrested for having stills.[226] Much of the liquor being sold was by small-time bootleggers on a very local level. There were stories of many bootleggers who were caught, but it is likely that for every one who was there were many others who escaped the law.

The newspapers dutifully recorded the arrest of bootleggers, starting from almost the beginning of Prohibition. Just a few months after Columbus went dry, Anne Pettigrew was found guilty of selling liquor in the dry zone around Columbus Barracks.[227] This was a pretty clear-cut case—as part of the Wartime Prohibition Act, which had not been repealed yet, there were dry zones surrounding army barracks. Other cases were a bit stranger.

One from May 1919 told of how a man was charged eighty-eight dollars for two pints of whiskey after following women to a home on Cherry Street. Police were said to be investigating. What is odd is that it appears that the man who bought the illicit liquor went to the police to complain about the high cost.[228]

One thing that is clear from newspaper articles during the early years of Prohibition was that Wayne Wheeler did appear to have been correct about one thing: the costs of getting caught breaking the Prohibition laws were far too inadequate. Take the case of Ray Zimmerman, who was found guilty of selling liquor, violating wartime prohibition, to a man he said claimed to have been in great pain. The judge did not find the defense credible, but the fine was only $1 plus costs.[229] Other times, the fines could be a bit steeper. George Zarick, who operated a moonshine still, had to pay a $100 fine and serve two months in jail.[230] Even those who could legally sell alcohol were not immune to the temptation of making an extra dollar on the side when they could. Druggist Chester F. Hively holds the distinction for being the first Columbus citizen arrested for violating the Federal Prohibition Act. His crime was not labeling a bottle of alcohol he sold.[231] Druggists held an interesting position during Prohibition. With proper prescriptions, they were legally allowed to dispense alcohol, and as soon as Prohibition took effect, they saw a rapid increase in customers. Often the medicines they sold contained high amounts of alcohol.

By 1925, the Anti-Saloon League was able to get stricter penalties for bootlegging passed through Congress. The fines for violating Prohibition laws were much higher in 1925 than they had been at the beginning. Seven people were arrested for public intoxication in February 1925, and their fines were between $200 and $400, much higher than the single dollar charged at the beginning. One man was arrested when fifty half-pint bottles were seized during a raid; his fine was $750.[232]

During Prohibition, there were other crimes more sinister than just bootlegging. One of the most tragic crimes during Prohibition was the proliferation of tainted alcohol and the sale of other poisonous concoctions. During Prohibition, many people turned to whatever they could to get drunk. In one of the most despicable acts, human greed and our own government allowed poisoned alcohol and alcoholic substitutes to get into the market. The consequences of drinking the tainted alcohol were profound, as some people went blind, were paralyzed or even died.

There are purposes for alcohol other than drinking. Alcohol frequently had industrial uses as a solvent. To make the industrial (or denatured)

Jamaica Ginger label. *Courtesy of the Library of Congress.*

alcohol, chemicals were added that were supposed to render it undrinkable.[233] Early in Prohibition, the Anti-Saloon League floated the idea that all the distilleries should denature their stockpiles of liquor—the distillers could still make a profit from their alcohol, but no one would be drinking it. The problem with denaturing alcohol was that the additional chemicals did not actually stop people from drinking it. Aware that people were turning to industrial alcohol to get drunk, the federal government took tragic and brutal steps to ensure that the practice would not continue. It was decided that the way to stop people from drinking industrial alcohol was to give it poisonous additives.[234] To make the industrial alcohol more poisonous, methanol, or wood alcohol, was added. Methanol is extremely toxic; even small doses can cause blindness, while larger doses can kill.

Poisoned alcohol did eventually make it to Columbus. One particularly dramatic instance was reported in the *Dispatch*. It began when "a drunken man staggered from the rear of a downtown house and yelled 'there's a dead man in that house.'" It seemed that Charles Reinerd had found Tor Peterson dead in his bed and his wife, Ada, dead in their attic. Mrs. Reinerd told the *Dispatch*, "When Tor came home drunk Ada would start drinking too. Sometimes he would beat her and she would run to the attic to hide." A man named Joseph Foley who visited the Petersons died at his home the next day. Bottles were found scattered everywhere in the Foleys' home, and one had a label that read, "Completely denatured alcohol."[235] In a city the size of Columbus, it is probable that there were more than just these three people who died from ingesting the toxic drink.

In a disgusting turn for the Anti-Saloon League, its leaders actually supported the poisoning of alcohol. Wayne Wheeler was quoted as saying that "the Government is under no obligation to furnish the people with alcohol that is drinkable when the Constitution prohibits it. The person who drinks this industrial alcohol is a deliberate suicide....To root out a bad habit costs many lives and long years of effort."[236] Wheeler actually made the claim that government should be allowed to deliberately poison alcohol and justified his extreme stance by claiming that the few lives it costs pale in comparison to the many who died because of alcohol before Prohibition. It was a strange turn of events that the Anti-Saloon League, once a bastion of morality, was now openly advocating the government be allowed to indirectly kill American citizens.

Denatured alcohol was not the only dangerous drink that people turned to during Prohibition. Another dangerous one was a patent medicine known as Jamaica Ginger, which was able to be sold legally during Prohibition, although it was expensive. Because of its expense, bootleggers tried to make their stocks go further and began to add various chemicals to the extract. These new additions happened to cause severe nerve damage and left thousands of people paralyzed.[237] It is unclear how bad the situation was in Columbus regarding Jamaica Ginger, but people were using it here. In October 1920, thieves stole a supply from Columbus Physicians and Druggists Supply Company one Wednesday night. The next day, the thieves went back to steal some more.[238] As Prohibition started to wear on, situations got desperate for drinkers as they turned to poison to cure their thirst.

Seized liquor. *Courtesy of the Library of Congress.*

Beyond the victims of poisoned alcohol, there were other lives lost in the city during Prohibition. Just because there were no gangsters in Columbus did not mean that there was no violent crimes. People can and did hurt and kill. Three police officers were killed in the line of duty trying to enforce Prohibition laws. This might not be as many as in other cities, but their lives still meant a great deal. The first officer to be killed was detective Charles Tiller, who had recently been promoted to the city's plainclothes division. On October 19, 1920, according to the *Columbus Dispatch*, "Detective Charles Tiller [was] shot by bootlegger John Cooper in the soft drink parlor of Edward Noble at Maple and Armstrong streets. Tiller was about to search Cooper, who he determined to have brought home brew into the parlor, when he was shot."[239]

The day after the shooting, a "$500 dollar reward offered for the arrest of Det. Tiller's killer." It was also reported that "police believe that the killer is still in Columbus."[240] Cooper was not actually still in Columbus, although his time on the lam only lasted a day. The next day, the headlines declared "John Cooper Captured: Declares to His Captors that He Is Not Sorry He Killed Charles E. Tiller." Newspapers at the time were much more sensational than they are today. The story continued: "Thrilling Chase, Culminating in Hot Fight, Reads Like a Wild Western Story." Cooper was found south of Athens and cornered by officers. "Officers spread out a distance of 15 feet apart and started in a pincher movement through the thicket….Cooper turned in time to discover them at a distance of more than 150 yards from his vantage point on a knoll." Then "he lowered himself to the ground and lying on this stomach he opened fire" with the automatic pistol with which he shot Charles Tiller in one hand and a Colt .38 revolver in the other. Cooper "kept up a continual fire of so accurate a range that the officers feared to approach further." Cooper pretended to run out of ammo so officers would creep closer. Eventually, the officers managed to surround Cooper by crawling up the hill and wound him before taking him into custody. During the hour-and-a-half-long gunfight, Cooper grazed an officer and was "slightly scratched by buckshot."[241]

Four months later, the second officer was killed. On February 26, 1921, Jesse Reall, after his wife begged him not to, volunteered to join a shift on the police liquor squad. It was supposed to be a simple search. Reall found whiskey in the car but was shot twice by Pomp Brooks.[242] There was a strange twist in the Reall case, as Reall's boss, Corporal Baker, the head of the liquor squad, was suspended due to allowing Reall to take a bottle of wine from the basement of the grocery that they raided before the shooting. Later, the bottle of wine could not be found.[243] It is possible that even the liquor squad was not entirely on the level.

Following the shootings, 244 Columbus police officers took a onetime two-dollar deduction of pay to go to help the widows of Charles Tiller and Jesse Reall.[244]

The last officer who was killed was possibly the most tragic. W.O. "Spike" Womeldorf actually was killed during a gun battle. Unlike gunfights in the movies, there was nothing glamorous about this one. The consequences were tragic and bloody. The fight began when federal Prohibition agents raided the house of a suspected bootlegger named Alanzo Thomas. During the raid, Thomas tried to give the federal agents the slip, but they gave chase. Officer Womeldorf happened to be raiding the house of Thomas's mother (and found alcohol) when he received the call that Thomas was fleeing federal agents. Unfortunately for Womeldorf, Thomas and the federal agents happened to converge on Thomas's mother's house. The shootout began after Thomas was caught off guard by the presence of Womeldorf. From there, everything went wrong. It was not a fight that should have gone Thomas's way, as there were officers from multiple agencies, including the Columbus and Bexely police as well as the federal government. In the heat of battle, mistakes were made. Constable Albert Haines of Bexely was hit in the leg, and a four-year-old bystander was hit in the shoulder. Officer Womeldorf was struck and killed by fire from the federal Prohibition agents. Thomas got away.

Murder victims during Prohibition were not just police officers. And crimes committed were not limited to bootleggers and other traditional criminals. On March 14, 1928, there was found a dead man in the office of Columbus city treasurer Elmer E. Jenkins at city hall. The man was named Clement Walter, and just how he ended up dead in the treasurer's office was the mystery. In part, it came about because Prohibition did not work. Jenkins and Walter were at city hall because of a party. Perhaps one should expect that those in positions of power would follow the laws that some of them helped to put in place, but the story of Prohibition is partially a story of hypocrisy. Parties at the Columbus City Hall were apparently not of the dry variety.

The night of March 14, 1928, Jenkins and Walter invited two women to go to city hall, which had been long rumored to have been a site for drunken debauchery. The night ended with Walter dead. Apparently, after the two unidentified women left, Walter killed himself—at least, that was the story that the treasurer initially told the police. But it was not true. After being questioned, Jenkins changed his story. When the party was over, the second story went, Jenkins and Walter went back to Jenkins's office, where Walter "suddenly and without warning" took the gun that Jenkins, for some reason, had in a drawer in his desk. "I'll plug you," said Walter before shooting and missing. There was a struggle for the gun, during which it went off, striking and killing Jenkins. Wondering what to do, Jenkins decided "to try to cover the thing up, so I grabbed the gun, put it in his right hand, and put his hand in his lap."[245] The outcome of this event was that the city council launched a probe into the "moral turpitude" at city hall. Strangely, there was no evidence found of the rumored wild parties.[246]

Without those who passed the laws respecting them, was there any hope that they were being enforced in any serious way? Looking back, it is obvious that Prohibition would not be around for much longer. The cracks were beginning to show, and once they became apparent, it was far too late to do anything to repair them.

Chapter 12

PROHIBITION COMES TO AN END

When we last heard from the Anti-Saloon League, it was 1925 and it was undergoing an internal civil war over its role during Prohibition. One faction, led by *American Issue* editor Ernest Cherrington, wanted to focus on education to convince people that Prohibition was in their best interests. The other side was led by General Counsel Wayne Wheeler, who believed that strict enforcement of Prohibition laws would coerce people into following them. Adding to the Anti-Saloon League's problems was the fact that funding had been drying up since 1920.

By 1925, although it did not yet know it, the Anti-Saloon League's days as a force to be reckoned with were numbered. A key factor in the decline of the Anti-Saloon League was the 1924 resignation of Purley Baker from the general superintendent position. Prior to the election of the new superintendent, it was assumed that Cherrington was a shoo-in for the position. As the editor of all the Anti-Saloon League literature for more than a decade, Cherrington had been the one who oversaw much of the league's public outreach, and he was also quite popular with the state-level organizations. Cherrington was not popular, however, with Wayne Wheeler and Anti-Saloon League founder Howard Russell.

Both Wheeler and Russell viewed Cherrington's belief in the power of education to be overly idealistic and unrealistic. Both believed that the only way to ensure the success of Prohibition was through heavy-handed enforcement. Cherrington did not seem to realize that despite being the editor of the league's propaganda, it was Wheeler who was viewed as

Anti-Prohibition forces were gaining strength. *Courtesy of the Library of Congress.*

being the league's public face. It was Wheeler who fought on Capitol Hill and issued releases to the newspapers. Wheeler also seemed to revel in the limelight and power that came with it. Unlike Cherrington, Wheeler did not actually run for the general superintendent position himself. Rather, he wanted a weak individual he could control to take the position.[247] Having a puppet working for him in Westerville would enable Wheeler to maintain his role as the general counsel, meaning that he could still be wheeling dealing in Washington.

Cherrington was so confident that he would be able to a of general superintendent that he did not even campaign fo

Through underhanded machinations, Wheeler and Russell were able to get former Illinois state superintendent and Wheeler ally Francis McBride elected. In the end, Wheeler got what he wanted, as McBride steered the league toward a policy of backing strict law enforcement. Cherrington found himself working for a league that had turned hostile to his own beliefs, and he was left wondering how the league would be able to survive. "I AM ANXIOUS regarding its [the Anti-Saloon League's] future," he said in 1926, adding that Superintendent McBride and Wheeler wanted the league to be "majoring on enforcement, but yet need a world of education."[248] Cherrington was correct to question the ability of the Anti-Saloon League to survive during its civil war. By the mid-1920s, opposition to Prohibition was growing.

Unfortunately for the Anti-Saloon League, the rifts within the organization had been exposed during the fight over the general superintendent position. Wheeler became more and more emboldened, but his ego soon cost him his favor with the league. Wheeler's laser-like focus on tough enforcement and his penchant for always looking to gain more power soon put him at odds with the league as a whole. By 1927, Wheeler appeared to stop even pretending that he cared what the rest of the league thought and began to issue announcements and start programs that were unapproved by the league's governing bodies.[249]

Wheeler abruptly died in the summer of 1927, leaving a void in the leadership of the Anti-Saloon League. In the wake of Wheeler's death, Cherrington's position was slightly vindicated, though perhaps too late to put things back together. Following the death of Wheeler, there was a meeting of business, religious and league leaders to discuss the future of the organization. It was decided that the direction of the league since 1919 had been all wrong and that it should chart a course dedicated to education.[250] Instead of regrouping after Wheeler's death, however, the rest of the year was spent refighting the old battles. In the end, the league decided to restructure with two superintendents. McBride was retained as general superintendent, but Cherrington would be superintendent of education, publicity and research.

It was too little too late. By this time, it had become obvious that the league no longer wielded the power it once had.[251] Weakened, the league was unable to hold back the tide of anti-Prohibition sentiment that had been developing while it was focused on its own internal divisions. Without the Anti-Saloon League to act as a bulwark against the wet forces, it was only a matter of time before Prohibition would be over. Prohibition's failure, though, cannot rest solely on the shoulders of the Anti-Saloon League. To do so would ascribe it more power than it ever had. There were other factors that compromised the chances of Prohibition's success that were beyond the control of the league. Among those factors was the fact that those who ran the government, sometimes even those who were supposed to be in charge of Prohibition enforcement, did not actually take it seriously.

We've seen many people flaunt the laws of Prohibition—speakeasy operators, bootleggers and murderers—but there were others still. Part of the reason why Prohibition failed was because those who had power were frequently not actually its allies. It was not possible for Prohibition to succeed if those responsible for creating and enforcing the laws did not take them seriously. The whole experiment was rotten from the beginning. Human penchant for vice, it appears, was stronger than the moral righteousness of the Anti-Saloon League and others like it. It was probably embarrassing to the league that in its home state, drinking went on at the highest levels in its capital city. It turns out that dry sentiment did not actually run that deep behind closed doors. Were lawmakers hypocrites who were willing to take away others' right to drink without giving it up themselves? It appears that they were. In Columbus's hotels, "attendants specialize in quick service and provide fairly good liqueur too."[252] It has been speculated that "there was probably more legislation done in hotels than there were ever in the Statehouse."[253]

In Columbus, there was a fair amount of corrupt behavior that probably worked to accelerate the deterioration of Prohibition. At nearly every level of government in Columbus, Prohibition laws were flaunted: "Public Utility lobbyist win[ed] and din[ed] staunch Anti-Saloon League followers," and "Liquor [was] consumed in the capital building itself to celebrate passage of measures drafted by Anti Saloon League leaders."[254] It would be hard to be more hypocritical than that. These were the same men who fought for Prohibition alongside the Anti-Saloon League. Perhaps the lawmakers only pretended to believe in the dry cause because they knew that winning over the Anti-Saloon League was the way to get into power, or perhaps they were simply hypocrites and did actually believe that temperance was best for society—just not for themselves. The stories of the parties that took place at the statehouse would probably have horrified the sanctimonious leaders of the Anti-Saloon League, as it was rumored that there were "Babylonian revels" complete with an abundance of booze and even nude dancers.[255] State lawmakers did not respect Prohibition, but there were even more damaging allegations that would help to undermine the image of Prohibition.

Being the capital of Ohio, Columbus was also the seat of the federal Prohibition enforcement commissioner. The commissioner was supposed to be the ultimate authority when it came to the enforcement of national Prohibition. The role of the commission, according to Wheeler, was to "enforce the 18th amendment.…Loyalty to Constitution means the enactment and enforcement of effective prohibition laws."[256] One would think that the federal Prohibition commissioner would be immune to the lure of the drink or the thrill of bootlegging. Ohio federal Prohibition director Joshua Russell, the man in charge of enforcing the Prohibition amendment for the state of Ohio, could not be bothered to follow the laws himself. In what is probably one of the most completely hypocritical acts during Prohibition in Columbus, Russell was indicted along with Chief Clerk Merle Copeland for illegally obtaining permits to sell whiskey. The newspapers told of how "unscrupulous business men with political pull procured thousands of gallons of whiskey for bootleg use."[257] With elected officials and law enforcement agents doing their best to undermine the success of Prohibition and the Anti-Saloon League in disarray, it was a wonder that Prohibition ever lasted as long as it did.

The Anti-Saloon League was powerless to turn the tides and do something about the public officials who failed to uphold the law. Its "funds dr[ied] up and the Anti-Saloon League [could] influence fewer elections."[258] Without money to spread its propaganda, the Anti-Saloon League was no longer able to convince the public that Prohibition was an idea worth fighting for. In the absence of the league, anti-Prohibition candidates were elected to office.

By 1931, the Anti-Saloon League had still not recovered from its infighting and the death of Wayne Wheeler when it was faced with a new crisis. The federal government released the Wickersham Commission report on the state of Prohibition, which found that "drinking had increased since 1920 and that Prohibition had corrupted the legal and political system while encouraging others to disrespect the law."[259] We have already seen this to be true. The legislators, government officials and law enforcement agents were actively subverting the Eighteenth Amendment. The Wickersham Commission report did not recommend that the Eighteenth Amendment be repealed, however, but rather recommended that enforcement for Prohibition be stepped up.

Regardless of the recommendations, the damage was done, and the public's confidence in Prohibition was deeply shaken. National

Prohibition limped on for another two years before it was finally repealed in 1933. Ohio voted for ratification of the Twenty-First Amendment, which would repeal the Eighteenth, in December 1934. Governor George White called for a special legislative session to repeal state dry laws and start a liquor commission following the vote to repeal national Prohibition. The "promised benefits of increased sobriety, less poverty and lower crime never materialized," he said, justifying the votes against Prohibition.[260] The "Great Experiment" was over. Now the city just had to pick up the pieces.

CHAPTER 13

WHAT NEXT?

As Ernest Cherrington noted in 1913, generations of temperance warriors had fought hard to bring about a national Prohibition. Back then, Cherrington claimed that all the previous temperance organizations had achieved nothing and that it was the Anti-Saloon League that would finally win the war. Cherrington and the league did, in fact, bring about national Prohibition, but what did they actually achieve? What exactly was the effect of national Prohibition, and what was going to happen afterward?

It might be a surprise, but some of the temperance organizations that long battled for Prohibition are actually still in existence, although they wield much less influence than they once did. The failure of Prohibition may have destroyed the power that the Woman's Christian Temperance Union and the Anti-Saloon League had in the days before the Eighteenth Amendment, but it did not actually kill them.

In the aftermath of Prohibition, the Woman's Christian Temperance Union tried to regroup and continue the fight against alcohol. In 1940, the Ohio branch bought a house on Broad Street in Columbus to be its headquarters that was supposed to "give prestige to the organization reflecting the permanency of our work and continuing to shine as a perpetual beacon light of temperance and prohibition in our capital city of Columbus." Needless to say, its perpetual beacon eventually went out. Columbus never went dry again. The house remained with the WCTU until 1998, when it was sold due to an inability to maintain it.[261] Although its influence is not what it used to be, the WCTU does still exist. Today's WCTU still speaks out against alcohol and other drugs but also does advocacy work for women's, children's and labor rights, among other social reforms.[262]

The Anti-Saloon League survived Prohibition, too. For years after Prohibition, the league limped along. During World War II, the league attempted to duplicate its successes from the First World War by whipping up anti-drinking sentiment, but its time had passed and the bid was not a success.[263] The league remained in Westerville until 1973, when it donated its headquarters to the city, leaving behind the largest collection of anti-alcohol literature in the world.[264] Today, the former headquarters is run by the Westerville Public Library and is a museum dedicated to those temperance warriors who brought about national Prohibition. You can still read the *American Issue*, that venerable tool of temperance propaganda that Cherrington edited for so long. The Anti-Saloon League is still operating, sort of. Now known as the American Council on Addiction and Alcohol Problems and based out of Birmingham, Alabama, the organization that once brought the liquor traffic to its knees is still operating and advocating against alcohol and other drugs.[265]

Prohibition had a devastating effect on the brewing industry in Columbus and the Brewery District. That is not to say there were no bright spots in the wake of Prohibition. After repeal, knowing that the

August Wagner began brewing beer as soon as Prohibition was repealed. *Courtesy of the German Village Society.*

118

In honor of the old Gambrinus Brewery. *Courtesy of the German Village Society.*

homebrew market would soon be collapsing because alcohol was going to be legal again, Wasserstrom began making draft beer coolers, which turned into a bar and restaurant installation business.[266]

August Wagner was eager to get back to making beer and managed to get the first permit to brew beer in Columbus following Prohibition.[267] In the aftermath, Wagner attempted to regain some of the esteem and reputation that the brewers had prior to the First World War by donating $10,000 to the Columbus Zoological Society for an elephant house (which is now gone). The August Wagner Breweries did not end with Wagner's death, in 1944. It continued for almost thirty more years. Upon Wagner's death, longtime Wagner executive Nellie Lenahan took over the presidency of the company. By this time, other breweries had reopened in Columbus, but Wagner's was by far the largest. By the time Lenahan died in 1953, the August Wagner Breweries actually was the last remaining Columbus brewery. After Lenahan's death, the reins of the Wagner brewery were then taken up by James Amento, with Helen Wagner, August's daughter, as the vice-president.

The Wagner brewery finally closed in 1974, one year after its old foe, the Anti-Saloon League, abandoned its Westerville headquarters. "Suspension of operations [meant that the] last locally owned brewery will place the Wagner name along with names like Hoster, Born, and Schlee in the city's brewing history," read the *Columbus Dispatch*'s obituary of the company.[268] The end of the Wagner brewery was certain by 1974, as the company owed $40,000 in back taxes and $600,000 on mortgages and only made 250,000 barrels of beer per year, a number that meant it was not able to keep up with more modern breweries. With the passage of the Wagner brewery, so, too, went the last locally owned brewery in Columbus for nearly twenty-five years.

Nellie Lenahan. *Courtesy of the German Village Society.*

Wagner Brewery in the 1970s. *Courtesy of the Columbus Metropolitan Library.*

Other breweries did survive Prohibition. The Washington Brewery reopened in 1933 and once again made beer. The Franklin Brewery reopened in 1934, although it closed its doors in 1952.[269] The Ohio Brewery reopened as a brewery in 1941, but it had shut down by the end of the decade.[270]

It must be said that while the closure of the Wagner brewery in 1974 meant that the last hometown brewery had shut down, it did not mean that there were no breweries left in the city. Anheuser-Busch opened a plant in Columbus in 1968, a site that from the outset was able to brew almost 2 million barrels of beer per year. It is easy to see why the Wagner brewery was not able to compete at first.[271] However, over the years, upgrades to the plant have allowed it to produce around 10 million barrels per year now.[272]

EPILOGUE

Prohibition had a profound impact on the landscape of Columbus, both culturally and physically, for decades after it ended. Prior to Prohibition, Columbus had a thriving drinking culture, led by the German brewers who operated in the Brewery District. Following Prohibition's repeal, the breweries never really came back, and only Wagner's remained open in the Brewery District. The Brewery District itself was left almost derelict from the exodus of former brewery workers. The Brewery District was almost abandoned, and its prospects seemed pretty bleak. Today, things are different. Starting in the late 1980s, developers, sensing a desire for more urban living space, began to renovate a number of buildings, including some of the old breweries. It was noted at the time that there was not a lot of hassle in relocating business tenants from those buildings because there was almost no one left there to begin with.[273]

By the early 1990s, a long-term "Brewery District Plan" had been created as a guide for the redevelopment. The plan paid homage to the history of the area and had the primary goal of preserving the architectural integrity of the district through the revitalization process. The goal was to create an area that was close to downtown where people could live and shop. There were plans for new housing and a shopping center along Front Street, where most of the breweries had been located.[274] In 1993, a Brewery District Commission was created by the city government to deal with the challenges faced by the Brewery District. The district has been a success story, though one that was fifty years in the making. Today, it is an active, vital part of the city. Luxury condominiums are now available in the same buildings where Nicholas Schlee and Conrad Born made their beer. A popular Metro Park now exists on the Whittier Peninsula where once there was a police impound lot. There has been a lot of development in the brewery district, but what about actual breweries?

At just about the same time the Brewery District began to revitalize, brewing returned to Columbus. In 1988, the Columbus Brewing Company opened, the first locally owned brewery since the closure of the Wagner Brewery in 1974.[275] It was microbrews that made beer popular in Columbus again. "Drinking patterns of Columbus are changing. The youth of Columbus are big into microbrews," said Scott Frances, who began carrying homebrew kits at the Wine Makers shop in 1974 and was the founding brewmaster at the Columbus Brewing Company.[276] Since the opening of the Columbus Brewing Company, almost two dozen microbreweries have opened in the Central Ohio area.[277] In addition to microbreweries, Columbus also boasts distilleries, wineries and a meadery. There have even been attempts to resurrect one of the venerable brands from Columbus's pre-Prohibition history—twice there have been attempts to bring the Hoster brand back from the dead. Opening in 1989, the Hoster Brewpub was one of the first microbreweries in the city. Although the Hoster Brewpub went out of business in 2000, there has more recently been another attempt to revive the lost brand by investors, including the great-great-grandson of Louis Hoster. In Columbus today, nearly one hundred years after Prohibition took effect, Hoster's signature beer Gold Top is available in limited quantities.

NOTES

Chapter 1

1. *Ohio Public Health Journal* 5: 711.
2. Betti and Sauer, *Historic Columbus Taverns*, 33.
3. Schlegel, *Lager and Liberty*, 61.
4. *Ohio Cultivator* 8, no. 1 (January 1, 1852).
5. Ibid., 378.
6. Ibid., 9 (1853): 301.
7. Ibid.
8. Ibid., 10 (1854): 46.
9. Epstein, *Politics of Domesticity*.
10. Kerr, *Organized for Prohibition*, 37.
11. *Advance Guard* 1, no 1: 1.

Chapter 2

12. Kerr, *Organized for Prohibition*, 44.
13. *Columbus Dispatch*, "Only Survivor of Early Crusade Lives to See Victory."
14. Ibid.
15. Kerr, *Organized for Prohibition*, 46.
16. Temperance and Prohibition Papers, minutes of the First Annual Convention of the WCTU.
17. Ibid., minutes of the Fourth Annual Meeting of the National Woman's Christian Temperance Union, 138.
18. Kerr, *Organized for Prohibition*, 46.

19. Ibid., 50.
20. Ibid., 65.
21. Ibid., 57.
22. Ibid., 61.
23. Ibid., 71.

Chapter 3

24. Sheban, "How Dry We Were."
25. Cherrington, *History of the Anti-Saloon League*, 7.
26. Ibid., 10.
27. Ibid., 43.
28. Ibid., 44.
29. Ibid., 12.
30. Ibid., 13.
31. Kerr, *Organized for Prohibition*, 77.
32. Ibid., 73.
33. Ibid.
34. Gold, *Democracy in Session*, 207.
35. Cherrington, *History of the Anti-Saloon League*, 62.
36. Kerr, *Organized for Prohibition*, 85.
37. Syzmanski, *Pathways to Prohibition*, 186.
38. Ibid., 187.
39. Kerr, *Organized for Prohibition*, 84; Cherrington, *History of the Anti-Saloon League*, 22.
40. Kerr, *Organized for Prohibition*, 99.
41. Ibid., 87.
42. Cherrington, *History of the Anti-Saloon League*, 38.
43. Kerr, *Organized for Prohibition*, 125.
44. Ibid., 24.
45. Ibid., 100.
46. Ibid., 112.

Chapter 4

47. Schlegel, *Lager and Liberty*, 4.
48. Ibid., 3.
49. Dawson, *History of the L. Hoster Brewery of Columbus Ohio.*
50. *Brewery District Plan*, 7.
51. Schlegel, *Lager and Liberty*, 3.

52. *Brewery District Plan*, 8.

53. Schlegel, *Lager and Liberty*, 5; *Brewery District Plan*, 8.

54. Schlegel, *Lager and Liberty*, 5.

55. Ibid., 39.

56. Ibid., 38.

57. Ibid., 29.

58. Dawson, *History of the L. Hoster Brewery of Columbus Ohio*, 7.

59. Schlegel, *Lager and Liberty*, 49.

60. Ibid.

61. Conte, *German Village*, 12.

62. Lee, *History of Columbus*, vol. 1, 916.

63. Dawson, *History of the L. Hoster Brewery of Columbus Ohio*, 8.

64. Schlegel, *Lager and Liberty*, 12.

65. Ibid., 14.

66. Ibid.

67. Ibid.

68. Taylor, *Centennial History of Columbus*, vol. 1, 704.

69. Ibid., 749.

70. Lee, *History of Columbus*, vol. 2, 709.

71. Taylor, *Centennial History of Columbus*, vol. 2, 359.

72. Schlegel, *Lager and Liberty*, 23.

73. Ibid., 28.

74. Ibid., 28–29.

75. Taylor, *Centennial History of Columbus*, vol. 1, 568.

76. Ibid.

77. Ibid.

78. *Western Brewer* 51, no. 1 (1918): 4.

79. Darbee, *German Columbus*, 68.

80. Schlegel, *Lager and Liberty*, 38.

81. Betti and Sauer, *Historic Columbus Taverns*, 68; Schlegel, *Lager and Liberty*, 39.

82. Conte, *German Village*, 16.

83. Ibid., 13.

84. *Columbus Dispatch*, "Neighbor News: German Village."

Chapter 5

85. Schlegel, *Lager and Liberty*, 64.

86. Taylor, *Centennial History of Columbus*, vol. 1, 564.

87. Kerr, *Organized for Prohibition*, 127.

88. Cherrington, *History of the Anti-Saloon League*, 63.

89. Kerr, *Organized for Prohibition*, 113.

90. *Annals of the American Academy of Political and Social Sciences* 32, no. 3, "Regulation of the Liquor Traffic," 20.

91. Kerr, *Organized for Prohibition*, 166.

92. Ibid., 121.

93. Cherrington, *History of the Anti-Saloon League*, 110.

94. Kerr, *Organized for Prohibition*, 126, 151.

95. Sheban, "How Dry We Were."

96. *American Brewers Review* 20: 9.

97. Ibid., 368.

98. Schlegel, *Lager and Liberty*, 60.

99. Foster, *Brief History of the Breweries of German Village*, 11.

Chapter 6

100. Kerr, *Organized for Prohibition*, 137.

101. Ibid., 142.

102. Ibid.

103. Ibid., 143.

104. Ibid., 110.

105. Ibid., 144.

106. Ibid., 155.

107. *Columbus Dispatch*, "Drys Will Continue Anti Liquor Crusade."

108. Kerr, *Organized for Prohibition*, 158.

109. Schlegel, *Lager and Liberty*, 61.

110. Ibid., 65.

111. Ibid.

112. Kerr, *Organized for Prohibition*, 99.

113. Graichen, *Remembering German Village*, 105.

114. Schlegel, *Lager and Liberty*, 67.

115. Kerr, *Organized for Prohibition*, 156.

116. Darbee, *German Columbus*, 68.

117. Taylor, *Centennial History of Columbus*, vol. 1, 565.

118. Kerr, *Organized for Prohibition*, 207.

119. Ibid., 219.

120. Schlegel, *Lager and Liberty*, 61.

121. Ibid., 64.

122. *Western Brewer* 50, no. 5 (1918): 192.

123. Kerr, *Organized for Prohibition*, 202.

124. Ibid., 203.

125. Ibid., 202.

126. Ibid., 205.

127. Ibid., 296.

Chapter 7

128. Tebben, "Columbus Mileposts: May 27, 1919."

129. *Columbus Dispatch*, "Drys to Celebrate Recent Victories."

130. Ibid., "WCTU Meeting in Columbus for Annual Session."

131. Ibid.

132. Hooper, *History of the City of Columbus*, 100.

133. *Columbus Dispatch*, "Monday to Find Small Vent."

134. Betti and Sauer, *Historic Columbus Taverns*, 69.

135. *Columbus Dispatch*, "Monday to Find Small Vent."

136. Betti and Sauer, *Historic Columbus Taverns*, 97; Stallings, "Wet and Dry."

137. *Columbus Dispatch*, "Dry Days See Many Changes."

138. Anti-Saloon League, *Yearbook*, 1921, 264–65.

139. Stallings, "Wet and Dry."

140. Tebben, "Columbus Mileposts: May 27, 1919."

141. Pramik, "Fixture in the Restaurant Trade."

142. *Columbus Dispatch*, "Home Brews Not Allowed."

143. Bernard, *Revealed*, 89.

144. Tebben, "Ohio Milepost: 10/21/1906—Booze Masquerades as Medicine."

145. Meyers and Walker, *Wicked Columbus*, 36.

146. Tebben, "Ohio Milepost: 10/21/1906—Booze Masquerades as Medicine."

Chapter 8

147. Kerr, *Organized for Prohibition*, 219.

148. Ibid., 241.

149. Ibid., 246.

150. Ibid.

151. Ibid., 255.
152. Ibid.
153. Ibid., 144.
154. Ibid.
155. Ibid., 240.
156. Ibid., 230.
157. Ibid., 220.
158. Okrent, *Last Call*, 41.
159. *Columbus Dispatch*, "Drys to Celebrate Recent Victories."
160. Ibid., "Prohibition Code Is Needed."
161. Ibid., "Drys for World Organization."
162. *World League Against Alcoholism*, pamphlet.
163. Kerr, *Organized for Prohibition*, 220.
164. Ibid., 246.
165. Ibid.
166. *Columbus Dispatch*, "Anti Saloon Men to Take Program."
167. Ibid., "Chief Will Endeavor."
168. Ibid., "Congress' Power to Limit Alcohol."
169. Ibid., "Drys to Celebrate Recent Victories"; "Wheeler Tells What Dry Code Will Prohibit."
170. Kerr, *Organized for Prohibition*, 225.

Chapter 9

171. Gold, *Democracy in Session*, 304.
172. *Columbus Dispatch*, "Congress' Power to Limit Alcohol."
173. Ibid., "Monday to Find Small Vent."
174. Ibid.
175. Betti and Sauer, *Historic Columbus Taverns*, 97.
176. Hunter, *Historic Guidebook of Old Columbus*, 163.
177. Betti and Sauer, *Historic Columbus Taverns*, 108.
178. Benton, "Classic Columbus Haunts."
179. Stallings, "Wet and Dry"; Clark, *German Village*, 119.
180. Betti and Sauer, *Historic Columbus Taverns*, 131.
181. Ibid.

Chapter 10

182. *Western Brewer* 53, no. 3 (1919).
183. Hooper, *History of the City of Columbus*, 99.
184. *Columbus Dispatch*, "Four Breweries Are Undecided."
185. Foster, *Brief History of the Breweries of German Village*, 9.
186. *Columbus Dispatch*, "Four Breweries Are Undecided."
187. Graichen, *Remembering German Village*, 67.
188. *Western Brewer* 53, no. 3 (1919): 80; 53, no. 1 (1919): 31.
189. Ibid., 53, no. 1 (1919): 31.
190. Darbee, *German Columbus*, 75.
191. Dawson, *History of the L. Hoster Brewery of Columbus Ohio*, 11.
192. *Columbus Dispatch*, January 30, 1924.
193. Schlegel, *Lager and Liberty*, 49.
194. Conte, *German Village*, 5.
195. *German Village Booster*, March 4, 1988.
196. Graichen, *Remembering German Village*, 33.

Chapter 11

197. Stallings, "Wet and Dry."
198. *Ohio State Journal*, May 13, 1937.
199. Tebben, "Columbus Mileposts: 5/13/1937."
200. Ibid.
201. *Ohio State Journal*, May 13, 1937.
202. Ibid.
203. Anti-Saloon League, *Yearbook*, 1921, 266.
204. Ibid.
205. *Columbus Dispatch*, "Big Falling Off in Intoxicating Cases."
206. Anti-Saloon League, *Yearbook*, 1921, 266.
207. Ibid.
208. *Columbus Dispatch*, "Modern Officers Must Be Intelligent."
209. Ibid., "Chief Will Endeavor."
210. Ibid., "Drinks Whisky: Jailed."
211. Ibid., "College...Today and Way Back When."
212. Kerr, *Organized for Prohibition*, 228.
213. Tebben, "Columbus Mileposts: June 13, 1929."
214. *Columbus Dispatch*, "Liquor License Suit to Be Filed Monday."

215. Ibid., "No Partiality to Be Shown."

216. *Columbus Dispatch*, "Draws Heavy Sentence"; Tebben, "Columbus Mileposts: 3/19/1928."

217. *Columbus Dispatch*, June 16, 1919.

218. Ibid., January 30, 1920.

219. Ibid., "Evidence Disappears."

220. Ibid., "Federal Agents on Trail."

221. Ibid., "Reformatory Trustees in League"; "Boy Arrested with Parents."

222. Ibid., "Home Brews Not Allowed."

223. Ibid., "Bootlegger of Savannah Testifies."

224. Ibid., "Paid Riehl 10500."

225. *Ogdenville (NY) Republic Journal*, March 1, 1927.

226. *Columbus Dispatch*, "More Arraigned in District Court."

227. Ibid., "Sold Liquor Against Law."

228. Ibid., "Liquor $44 a Pint."

229. Ibid., "'Framed' Bootlegger Cases."

230. Ibid., "Operator of Still Is Given Sentence."

231. Ibid., "Druggist Denies Guilt."

232. Ibid., "Liquor Violators Are Given Heavy Fines."

233. Rothman, "History of Poisoned Alcohol."

234. Ibid.

235. Tebben, "Columbus Mileposts: June 13, 1929."

236. Okrent, *Last Call*, 289.

237. Carson, *Silent Spring*, 197.

238. *Columbus Dispatch*, "Thieves Call Again."

239. Ibid., "Detective Slain by Bootlegger."

240. Ibid., "$500 Reward for Slayer's Arrest."

241. Ibid., "Negro Who Slew Police Officer."

242. Ibid., "Police Search for Slayer."

243. Ibid., "Officer Baker Suspended."

244. Tebben, "Columbus Mileposts: Feb 26, 1921."

245. Ibid., "Columbus Mileposts: May 27, 1919."

246. Ibid.

Chapter 12

247. Kerr, *Organized for Prohibition*, 233.

248. Ibid., 236.

249. Ibid., 238.
250. Ibid., 239.
251. Ibid., 240.
252. Gold, *Democracy in Session*, 408.
253. Stallings, "Wet and Dry."
254. Gold, *Democracy in Session*, 408.
255. Ibid., 408.
256. *Columbus Dispatch*, "Prohibition Code Is Needed."
257. *Evening Independent*, "Federal Judge Indicts Ten."
258. Kerr, *Organized for Prohibition*, 255.
259. Ibid., 260.
260. Tebben, "Ohio Milepost: 12/5/1934."

Chapter 13

261. *Columbus Dispatch*, "Temperance Union Puts Old House."
262. Woman's Christian Temperance Union, "Early History."
263. Kerr, *Organized for Prohibition*, 282.
264. Jarmon, "Westerville."
265. American Council on Addiction and Alcohol Problems, "Current Issues."
266. Pramik, "Fixture in the Restaurant Trade."
267. *Citizen Journal*, "Wagner Is First to Get Permit."
268. *Columbus Dispatch*, "Beer Making to End."
269. *Ohio State News*, April 7, 1952.
270. Foster, *Brief History of the Breweries of German Village*, 9.
271. *Upper Arlington News*, October 15, 2013.
272. Ibid.

Epilogue

273. *German Village Booster*, March 4, 1988.
274. *Brewery District Plan*, 3.
275. Armon, *Ohio Breweries*, 84.
276. *Columbus Dispatch*, "Business Is Hopping."
277. Malone, "Beer Expert Planning on Resurrecting Old Hoster."

BIBLIOGRAPHY

The Advance Guard 1, no. 1 (1872). Washington, D.C.: Henry Polkinhorn and Company.

American Brewers Review 20 (January–December 1906).

American Council on Addiction and Alcohol Problems. "Current Issues." http://sapacap.com/the-american-issue.

The Annals of the American Academy of Political and Social Sciences 32, no. 3. "Regulation of the Liquor Traffic" (November 1908).

Armon, Rick. *Ohio Breweries*. Mechanicsburg, PA: Stackpole Books, 2009.

Bernard, Meghan Leigh. *Revealed: Columbus, the Story of Us*. Wilmington, OH: Orange Frazer Press, 2013.

Betti, Tom, and Doreen Uhas Sauer. *Historic Columbus Taverns: The Capital City's Most Storied Saloons*. Charleston, SC: The History Press, 2012.

Brewery District Plan. Downtown Columbus Inc. Columbus, OH: Columbus Planning Division, 1992.

Carson, Rachel. *Silent Spring*. Boston: Houghton Mifflin, 1962.

Cherrington, Ernest. *History of the Anti-Saloon League*. Westerville, OH: American Issue Publishing Company, 1913.

Clark, John. *German Village: Stories Behind the Bricks*. Charleston, SC: The History Press, 2015.

Conte, Jean. *German Village*. Woodland Park, CO: Mountain Automation Corp., 1994.

Darbee, Jeffrey. *German Columbus*. Charleston, SC: Arcadia Publishing, 2005.

Dawson, Esther Hoster. *History of the L. Hoster Brewery of Columbus Ohio.* Columbus, OH: self-published, 1981.

Epstein, Barbara Leslie. *The Politics of Domesticity: Women, Evangelism, and Temperance in Nineteenth-Century America.* Middletown, CT: Wesleyan University Press, 1986.

Foster, Wayne David. *A Brief History of the Breweries of German Village.* Columbus, OH: self-published, 1987.

Gold, David. *Democracy in Session: A History of the Ohio General Assembly.* Athens: Ohio University Press, 2009.

Graichen, Jody. *Remembering German Village: Columbus, Ohio's Historic Treasure.* Charleston, SC: The History Press, 2010.

Hooper, Osman. *History of the City of Columbus: From the Founding of Franklinton in 1797, through the World War Period, to the Year 1920.* Columbus, OH: Memorial Publishing, 1920.

Hunter, Bob. *A Historic Guidebook of Old Columbus: Finding the Past in the Present in Ohio's Capital.* Athens: Ohio University Press, 2012.

Kerr, K. Austin. *Organized for Prohibition: A New History of the Anti Saloon League.* New Haven, CT: Yale University Press, 1985.

Lee, Alfred. *History of the City of Columbus, Capital of Ohio.* Vol. 1. New York: Munsell and Company, 1892.

———. *History of the City of Columbus, Capital of Ohio.* Vol. 2. New York: Munsell and Company, 1892.

Meyers, David, and Elise Meyers Walker. *Wicked Columbus, Ohio.* Charleston, SC: The History Press, 2015.

Monthly Bulletin of the Ohio State Board of Health 5 (1915). Columbus, OH: F.J. Heer Printing Company.

Ohio Cultivator 8, no. 1 (1852). Columbus, OH.

Ohio Cultivator 9, no. 3 (1853), Columbus, OH.

Okrent, Daniel. *Last Call: The Rise and Fall of Prohibition.* New York: Scribner, 2010.

Rothman, Lily. "The History of Poisoned Alcohol Includes an Unlikely Culprit: The U.S. Government." *TIME*, January 14, 2015. http://time.com/3665643/deadly-drinking.

Schlegel, Donald. *Lager and Liberty: German Brewers of Nineteenth Century Columbus.* Columbus, OH: self-published, 2014.

Syzmanski, Ann-Marie. *Pathways to Prohibition: Radicals, Moderates, and Social Outcome Movements.* Durham, NC: Duke University Press, 2003.

Taylor, William. *Centennial History of Columbus and Franklin County.* Vol. 1. Chicago: S.J. Clarke Publishing, 1909.

———. *Centennial History of Columbus and Franklin County*. Vol. 2. Chicago: S.J. Clarke Publishing, 1909.

Temperance and Prohibition Papers. Minutes of the First Annual Convention of the Woman's Christian Temperance Union. Series III. Roll I. Annual Meeting Minutes.

———. Minutes of the Fourth Annual Convention of the Woman's Christian Temperance Union. Series III. Roll I. Annual Meeting Minutes.

Wasserstrom. "About Wasserstrom." http://www.wasserstrom.com/restaurant-supplies-equipment/corporate-info.

The Western Brewer and Journal of the Barley, Malt and Hops Trade 50, no. 5 (May 1918).

The Western Brewer and Journal of the Barley, Malt and Hops Trade 51, no. 1 (July 15, 1918).

The Western Brewer and Journal of the Barley, Malt and Hops Trade 53, no. 1 (July 1919).

The Western Brewer and Journal of the Barley, Malt and Hops Trade 53, no. 3 (September 1919).

Woman's Christian Temperance Union. "Early History." https://www.wctu.org/history.html.

World League Against Alcoholism. Pamphlet. Westerville, OH: American Issue Publishing Company, n.d.

NEWSPAPERS

Benton, G.A. "Classic Columbus Haunts: Ringside Café." *Columbus Alive*, October 6, 2010.

Citizen Journal. "Wagner Is First to Get Permit to Brew Beer After Prohibition." February 17, 1972.

Columbus Dispatch. "Anti Saloon Men to Take Program before Congress." October 17, 1920.

———. "Beer Making to End at Wagner Brewery." January 6, 1974.

———. "Big Falling Off in Intoxicating Cases." July 31, 1919.

———. "Bootlegger of Savannah Testifies He Paid Riehl for Prison Favors." February 10, 1925.

———. "Boy Arrested with Parents for Violating Liquor Laws." February 18, 1925.

————. "Business Is Hopping." March 3, 1997.

————. "Chief Will Endeavor to Locate 'Wet Spot.'" June 18, 1919.

————. "College…Today and Way Back When…Family Members Recall Days at OSU, Capital." December 1, 1991.

————. "Congress' Power to Limit Alcohol Held Clear." July 16, 1919.

————. "Detective Slain by Bootlegger." October 29, 1920.

————. "Draws Heavy Sentence." October 26, 1919.

————. "Drinks Whisky: Jailed." August 1, 1919.

————. "Druggist Denies Guilt." January 23, 1920.

————. "Dry Days See Many Changes." June 1, 1919.

————. "Drys for World Organization to Vanquish Liquor." June 7, 1919.

————. "Drys to Celebrate Recent Victories." June 10, 1919.

————. "Drys Will Continue Anti Liquor Crusade." January 12, 1920.

————. "Evidence Disappears." July 29, 1919.

————. "Federal Agents on Trail of Liquor Ring." January 24, 1925.

————. "$500 Reward for Slayer's Arrest." October 30, 1920.

————. "Four Breweries Are Undecided as to Future Plans." May 28, 1919.

————. "'Framed' Bootlegger Cases Frowned Upon." January 13, 1920.

————. "Franklin County Gives Dry Act Large Majority." November 4, 1920.

————. "Home Brews Not Allowed Under New Dry Laws." February 7, 1925.

————. January 30, 1920.

————. January 30, 1924.

————. June 16, 1919.

————. "Liquor $44 a Pint." August 3, 1919.

————. "Liquor License Suit to Be Filed Monday." May 29, 1919.

————. "Liquor Violators Are Given Heavy Fines." February 13, 1925.

————. "Many Violating Dry Laws White Charges." June 13, 1919.

————. "Modern Officers Must Be Intelligent." October 15, 1920.

————. "Monday to Find Small Vent in Prohibition Veil." May 24, 1919.

————. "More Arraigned in District Court." September 9, 1919.

————. "Negro Who Slew Police Officer Captured Near Athens, O. After Gun Battle with Sheriff's Posse." October 31, 1920.

————. "Neighbor News: German Village." September 2, 1987.

————. "No Partiality to Be Shown in Law Enforcement." January 16, 1920.

————. "Officer Baker Suspended by Chief French." March 1, 1921.

————. "Only Survivor of Early Crusade Lives to See Victory." January 16, 1920.

————. "Operator of Still Is Given Sentence." December 18, 1919.

————. "Paid Riehl 10500 Says Bootlegger Haas." February 11, 1925.

————. "Police Search for Slayer of Jesse Reall." February 27, 1921.

————. "Prohibition Code Is Needed Says Wheeler." June 1, 1920.

————. "Reformatory Trustees in League with Bootleggers." February 24, 1925.

————. "Reports Whisky Theft." January 30, 1920.

————. "Sartain and Riehl Face Court Monday." February 7, 1925.

————. "Sold Liquor Against Law." September 10, 1919.

————. "Temperance Union Puts Old House on the Market." February 27, 1998.

————. "Thieves Call Again." October 29, 1920.

————. "WCTU Meeting in Columbus for Annual Session." October 14, 1919.

————. "Wheeler Outlines Plan to Nab Bootleggers." June 10, 1919.

————. "Wheeler Tells What Dry Code Will Prohibit." July 27, 1919.

Evening Independent. "Federal Judge Indicts Ten in Huge Booze Conspiracy." February 28, 1925.

German Village Booster. March 4, 1988.

Jarmon, Josh. "Westerville: Reopened Cities Recall War, Dry Times." *Columbus Dispatch*, March 23, 2015.

Malone, JD. "Beer Expert Planning on Resurrecting Old Hoster." *Columbus Dispatch*, March 13, 2016.

Ogdenville (NY) Republic Journal. March 1, 1927.

Ohio State Journal. May 13, 1937.

Ohio State News. April 7, 1952.

Pramik, Mike. "A Fixture in the Restaurant Trade: Columbus' Wasserstrom Marks a Century of Service." *Columbus Dispatch*, September 22, 2002.

Sheban, Jeffrey. "How Dry We Were." *Columbus Dispatch*, September 25, 2011.

Stallings, Beth. "Wet and Dry." *Columbus Monthly*, January 2014.

Tebben, Gerald. "Columbus Mileposts: Feb 26, 1921—Bootleggers Bullets Cuts Down Policemen." *Columbus Dispatch*, February 26, 2012.

————. "Columbus Mileposts: 5/13/1937—Columbus Gambler Had Diamond Studs and a Heart of Gold." *Columbus Dispatch*, May 13, 2012.

————. "Columbus Mileposts: June 13, 1929—Bad Liquor a Killer in Prohibition." *Columbus Dispatch*, June 13, 2012.

————. "Columbus Mileposts: May 27, 1919—Drinks Were Lacking that Extra Kick." *Columbus Dispatch*, May 27, 2012.

———. "Columbus Mileposts: 3/19/1928—Man Killed at City Hall Boozefest." *Columbus Dispatch*, March 19, 2012.

———. "Ohio Milepost: 10/21/1906—Booze Masquerades as Medicine." *Columbus Dispatch*, October 21, 2003.

———. "Ohio Milepost: 12/5/1934—Ohio Ratifies Repeal of Prohibition." *Columbus Dispatch*, December 5, 2003.

Upper Arlington News. October 15, 2003.

INDEX